Mercedes SL Series

THE COMPLETE STORY

Other Titles in the Crowood AutoClassic Series

Mercedes SL Series

THE COMPLETE STORY

ANDREW NOAKES

CROWOOD

First published in 2004 by
The Crowood Press Ltd
Ramsbury, Marlborough
Wiltshire SN8 2HR

www.crowood.com

British Library Cataloguing-in-Publication Data
A catalogue record for this book is available from the British Library.

ISBN 1 86126 673 1

Typeset by Servis Filmsetting Ltd, Manchester

Printed and bound in Great Britain by CPI Bath

Contents

Mercedes-Benz SL Evolution 1952–2004

1951 – Daimler-Benz management approves a racing programme for 1952.

1952 – Hermann Lang and Fritz Riess win the Le Mans 24-hour race in a W194 SL. Later that year Karl Kling and Hans Klenk win the Carrera Panamericana.

1954 – Road-going 300SL 'Gullwing' and 190SL announced at the New York International Motor Sport Show.

1957 – Paul O'Shea wins the American Sports Car Championship for the third time in a Mercedes-Benz 300SL. Production of the Gullwing ends. Replaced by 300SL Roadster.

1963 – 230SL 'Pagoda' debuts at the Geneva show. Eugen Böhringer and Klaus Kaiser win Spa-Sofia-Liège rally in a 230SL.

1967 – 250SL replaces 230SL.

1968 – 280SL replaces 250SL.

1971 – 350SL and US-spec 350SL 4.5 replace the 'Pagoda-roof' SL. The hard-top SLC Coupé is added to the range.

1973 – 450SL introduced into Europe.

1974 – Six-cylinder 280SL added as a response to the oil crisis.

1977 – Alloy-block V8 engine debuts in the 450SLC 5.0.

1980 – Revisions for all models. Alloy-block V8s power new 380SL and 500SL models.

1981 – SLC replaced by the saloon-based SEC coupés.

1986 – Further revisions, including front air dams. New 300SL six-cylinder model and 420SL V8. 560SL for US market.

1989 – New R129SL launched at Geneva show with a choice of two six-cylinder engines and a 5.0-litre V8.

1992 – V12 600SL introduced

1993 – Daimler-Benz phases in new nomenclature, carrying the series letters before the engine designation. 600SL, for instance, becomes SL600. New four-valve six-cylinder engines in SL280 and SL320.

1996 – SLK is launched, returning Mercedes-Benz to the 190SL market segment.

1998 – New V6 engines replace the straight sixes.

1999 – AMG introduces high-performance V8 and V12 SLs.

2001 – R230 SL500 and SL55 AMG replace the R129 SL range.

2002 – SL350 and SL600 added to the range for the 2003 model year. Mercedes-Benz SLR-McLaren makes its debut.

2004 – New R171 SLK and SL65 AMG make their debuts.

Introduction

The three-pointed star of Mercedes-Benz adorns all kinds of vehicles, from trucks and taxis to luxury saloons and huge limousines. Sports cars, too, and for more than half a century the sporting side of the Mercedes-Benz range has been represented by a line of well-respected cars carrying a simple two-letter designation: SL.

Yet the five main generations of SL-class Mercedes, and the offshoots and derivatives they spawned, have spanned more than just the years. The SL has played many roles: there have been highly successful racing cars, accomplished roadsters, elegant coupés and genuine supercars. The SL has been powered by engines with six, eight and twelve cylinders, with power outputs ranging from 150bhp to more than 600bhp.

The SL has seen enormous changes in technology, too. Right from the start the SL has been at the forefront of automotive engineering, with such features as fuel injection and a spaceframe chassis as far back as the early fifties. Since then the SL-class has introduced Mercedes drivers to sophisticated suspensions, new tyre technology, innovative safety equipment and much more.

So the SL-class Mercedes is more than just a line of sporting cars. It is a fifty-year story of changing technology, developing markets and shifting perceptions of what makes a great driver's car – and what a sports car from Mercedes-Benz should be like. And it is also clear proof that, to the engineers behind these cars, the three-pointed star represents a continuing passion for perfection.

The original SL was built to win in sports-car racing, and succeeded in dominating the 1952 season. Subsequent SL road cars have been just as successful on the road.

1 The Marque of Quality

Mercedes-Benz cars are renowned for the quality of their engineering. Everything from the engine to the air vents, from the driveshafts to the door locks, has been meticulously designed, tested, redesigned, approved and then manufactured to a level of quality that is rarely seen in other cars. In a Mercedes you know everything will work, it will work well, and it will go on working – for many hundred-thousand miles.

This sound engineering and quality of manufacture have seen the Mercedes-Benz marque through to success with a wide range of products, from passenger cars to commercial vehicles, to tractors and off-road vehicles – even aero-engines. It was this same high-quality approach to design and production that would earn Mercedes-Benz supremacy in Grand Prix racing between the wars, and make a Mercedes the car of choice for the rich and famous the world over. It was that same philosophy that would return Mercedes-Benz to the pinnacle of motor sport less than ten years after the Second World War had reduced the company to rubble.

It's here, in the period of post-war reconstruction, that the SL enters the story, first as a racing car designed to put the Mercedes-Benz name back in the spotlight and, once that was achieved, as a road car that few manufacturers, if any, could match. But the origins of the company date back to the 1880s – the very earliest years of the motor car.

Origins of a marque

The company that would eventually build Mercedes-Benz cars was originally two separate concerns, founded by Karl Benz and Gottlieb Daimler towards the end of the nineteenth century. Benz, the son of a railway engine driver, studied engineering at Karlsruhe and set up his own business, Benz & Cie, at Mannheim in 1880. At first he made two-stroke stationary engines, but a rear-engined motorized tricycle followed in 1885 and, in January 1886, Benz was awarded a patent for his *motorwagen*. Meanwhile Daimler, the son of a baker, had served an apprenticeship to a gunmaker before working in a series of engineering firms and then, in 1872, joining Gasmotorenfabrik Deutz near Cologne. As technical director, Daimler worked with his chief engineer, Wilhelm Maybach, to refine the four-stroke engine that had been created by Deutz-founder Nikolaus Otto (after whom the four-stroke 'Otto cycle' is named), but eventually the pair found themselves at loggerheads with Otto over their new designs for 'high speed' engines. In 1882, Daimler and Maybach resigned from the Deutz company and set up in business for themselves. In a greenhouse behind Daimler's home in the Stuttgart suburb of Cannstatt, they further developed Daimler's engine and by 1886 had built a motorized coach.

Benz sold one of his motorized tricycles to Parisian engineer Emile Roger in 1887 and Roger became Benz's sales agent in France,

Gottlieb Daimler (left) and Karl Benz, founders of the two companies that would later build Mercedes-Benz cars.

where most early Benz vehicles would be sold. By the turn of the century, Benz & Cie was the biggest car maker in the world with total production exceeding 2,000 cars, but the company's designs – though now four-wheeled – still had much in common with the original tricycle of a decade before. Benz had started out as an innovator, but having found a successful design he was by no means willing to change it.

Keener to experiment with new designs, Daimler quickly moved away from producing cars that were little more than powered horse-carriages. In 1897, Daimler and Maybach transferred the engine from the rear of the car to the front, in the new twin-cylinder Phoenix, and then developed a faster front-engined car with an in-line four-cylinder engine at the behest of Emil Jellinek, Consul-General of the Austro-Hungarian empire in Nice, in the south of France. Jellinek acted as an unofficial dealer for Daimler cars, selling them to his wealthy friends and contacts. When the four-cylinder cars proved successful Jellinek requested even faster cars, which he promoted at the annual Nice speed trials. Jellinek believed these German cars would sell better in France with a less German-sounding

The Gottlieb Daimler Memorial in Bad Cannstatt preserves the site where the world's first high-speed gasoline engine was built in 1883. This is the tool bench in Daimler's workshop.

Emil Jellinek introduced the name 'Mercedes' on the Daimler cars he sold in France.

Mercédès Jellinek, daughter of Emil, whose name would become synonymous with high-quality automobiles.

name, so he called them 'Mercédès' after his ten-year-old daughter. But there was another reason for the change: Panhard-Levassor was importing Daimler engines into France to power its own cars and had acquired the French rights to the Daimler name.

Gottlieb Daimler died in 1900, but his company flourished and, to cope with strong demand, a larger factory was set up in the Untertürkheim district of Stuttgart in 1901. Maybach left the company in 1907 after clashing with Daimler's son Paul, who succeeded him as chief engineer. In 1909 a new logo was adopted: a three-pointed star, signifying that Daimler's engines were used on land, sea and in the air.

Benz had by now accepted that his company's car designs had to change and develop to keep up with the increasingly

sophisticated competition, and the new Parsifal model had rescued the company's fortunes. Benz cars, like Mercedes, were now involved in motor sport and the *Blitzen* Benz – an enormous 21-litre machine developing 200bhp – had broken the world land speed record, eventually raising it to 140.865mph (226.700km/h) in 1911. To celebrate Benz swapped its 'gear wheel' logo for a stylized laurel wreath.

Inevitably war work took over for both companies in 1914 and when hostilities ended in 1918 the shattered German economy left little domestic market for new cars. Exports were equally difficult – few foreigners wanted to buy from a country that had so recently fought against them – and the German motor industry crumbled. The two troubled companies realized they had to work together and, in May 1924, Benz and Daimler entered into a co-operative agreement. Two years later they

The 35hp Mercedes, seen here at the Nice speed trials in 1903, set the pattern for the development of the modern sports car.

Daimler's right-hand man Wilhelm Maybach was responsible for the design of the 35hp. After Daimler's death he split with the company and built cars under his own name.

merged. At first both marques retained their individual identities, but eventually they were combined into one and the company became known as Daimler-Benz Aktiengesellschaft (AG). The new company merged its logos, too, combining the Daimler three-pointed star with the Benz laurel wreath.

The Mercedes-Benz cars that the new company would make during the 1920s and 1930s would be masterminded by Daimler chief engineer Ferdinand Porsche and his successor Dr Hans Nibel, who had been chief engineer of Benz. Mercedes-Benz's luxury models would be chosen by celebrities and heads of state (including the exiled Kaiser Wilhelm II), while racing versions would become successful in the hands of such luminaries of the time as Rudolf Caracciola, Manfred von Brauchitsch and Hans Stuck.

The Daimler and Benz companies retained their separate identities even after they began working together to build Mercedes-Benz cars – but soon they would become one.

The Mercedes and Benz logos were brought together in the merger of 1926: today's three-pointed star is derived from a Daimler logo of the 1920s.

The Mercedes SSK was the car to beat in motor racing in the 1920s. The lightweight SSKL version was a distant ancestor of the SL.

Touring versions of the SSK were popular with millionaires and celebrities, such as German opera singer Richard Tauber.

Ever faster, heavier and more powerful, the colossal supercharged racing cars of the time culminated in the 7.1-litre SSKL, the designation standing for Super, Sports, *Kurz* meaning short and *Leicht* meaning (relatively) light weight. Extensive drilling of the chassis members reduced weight and the driver could engage a supercharger, which gave him more than 300bhp – but only for a few seconds at a time, or engine damage would ensue. But the SSKL and its ilk were difficult and dangerous beasts to drive, and in a bid to improve safety the motor racing authorities (at the time the AIACR, or Association Internationale des Automobiles Clubs Reconnus) introduced a new upper weight limit of 750kg for the 1934 season. Daimler-Benz responded with a radical new car.

The sophisticated W25 had all-independent suspension, hydraulic brakes, and a body shape clearly designed to cut wind resistance to the minimum. Its 3.4-litre straight-eight engine with four valves per cylinder developed more than 300bhp. The W25 was immediately successful, dominating Grand Prix racing in 1934, but Auto Union and Alfa Romeo quickly caught up and surpassed Mercedes-Benz until young engineer Rudolf Uhlenhaut was called in as part of a restructuring of the racing department; the result was a new line of 'Silver Arrows'. The W125, W154 and tiny 1.5-litre W163 would all contribute to Mercedes-Benz's domination of top-level motoring racing in the immediate pre-war years.

Then Daimler-Benz would become a major contributor to Germany's war effort – significantly as a manufacturer of fuel-injected aero-engines for *Luftwaffe* aircraft – and, as such, the company was an important target for Allied bombing campaigns. The devastating

The SSKL racing car took Rudolf Caracciola to the first 'foreign' win in the Mille Miglia. Note the drilled chassis rail just ahead of the rear wheels.

Mercedes-Benz and Auto Union fought for supremacy in Grand Prix racing in the 1930s. Caracciola's W125 triumphed at the Swiss GP in 1937.

effects of the war would bring Daimler-Benz to its knees.

Post-War Recovery

Daimler-Benz's three main factories around Stuttgart were almost totally destroyed by wartime bombing and car production did not restart until 1947. Even then, all that the factory was capable of building was a mildly updated version of the pre-war 170 saloon, but, later, more powerful engines and a 1.7-litre diesel were introduced. These made the 170 more popular and earned Daimler-Benz enough to invest in future models, the first of which would be aimed at a very different market: America.

The Uhlenhaut-designed W125 returned Mercedes-Benz to the top after a lean period. Here Lang stops for tyres and fuel on the way to winning at Avus in 1937.

52660

The W154 continued the success of the W125 into a new Grand Prix formula, which called for a supercharged V12 engine of no more than 3.0 litres.

The 170 saloon led the post-war reconstruction of Daimler-Benz: it was just about all the war-ravaged company was capable of making.

The new 300 series saloon that was Mercedes-Benz's attempt to win over the US market was unveiled at the first post-war Frankfurt Motor Show in April 1951. Modern styling, with integrated front wings and only vestigial running boards, marked it out from its pre-war predecessors, but under orders from Daimler-Benz chief Dr Wilhelm Haspel, the styling team led by Karl Wilfert had retained the characteristic Mercedes grille, giving the new car an imposing appearance. The new models were every bit as grand as the big Mercedes-Benz cars of the 1930s.

The 300's chassis followed Mercedes-Benz's pre-war practice, with two curved main members forming a backbone structure and incorporating all-independent coil-spring suspension, by double wishbones at the front and double-pivot swing axles at the back. Auxiliary torsion-bar springs at the back could be engaged by the driver, to keep the tail of the car level when carrying a full load. Lateral outriggers from the main chassis members carried unstressed bodywork, built at the Daimler-Benz Sindelfingen factory and available in a choice of saloon and four-door convertible configurations.

The engine, too, was derived from a pre-war design. The starting point was M159, a 2.6-litre straight-six engine that had been designed in the late thirties for a new 260 saloon. War had intervened before the 260 reached production, but the M159 engine had seen service in trucks and fire engines during the conflict. Now the straight-six was re-signed, with a wider bore and longer stroke to increase the swept volume from 2594cc to 2996cc, in which form it was redesignated M186. The new engine had a number of unusual features for the late 1940s, including inclined valves operated by an overhead cam-shaft, acting on 'finger' cam followers. The generous size of the valves promised excellent engine breathing. Another curious design feature was the sloping contact-surface between the cylinder block and the flat-faced head, the combustion chambers being formed with dished piston-crowns.

M186 proved to be a strong, smooth engine, which in its original form with twin downdraught carburettors developed 115bhp – despite a low compression ratio of 6.4:1 in deference to the poor quality fuels available in post-war Europe. It was enough to give the big 300 saloon a top speed of 96mph

(155km/h), and this 3,894lb (1,770kg) limousine could sprint to 60mph from rest in 18 seconds. Fuel consumption, if it mattered to an owner who would undoubtedly have been wealthy, was of the order of 17mpg (16ltr/100km).

The 300 was the biggest and fastest car that post-war Germany had yet produced and it found favour with heads of state, celebrities and VIPs all over the world. Architect Frank Lloyd Wright had one, as did film stars Yul Brynner and Gary Cooper, James Bond film producer Albert R. Broccoli and crooner Bing Crosby. Emperor Haile Selassie of Ethiopia and President Jawaharlal Nehru of India used 300s as their official cars, as did West German Chancellor Konrad Adenauer. Adenauer, in fact, was so attached to the 300 that he continued to use it until his death in 1967, long

Neubauer brought Mercedes back to motor sport with the pre-war W154s: Lang, Kling and Fangio line up for the start in Argentina.

18

86596

Kling wrestles the mighty W154 around the Buenos Aires track. Gonzales' Ferrari humbled the Mercedes team in both races.

after the 600 had taken over as Mercedes' ultimate saloon. The 300 is still popularly known as the 'Adenauer Mercedes' and the former Chancellor's final 300 is now in the collection at the Daimler-Benz Museum in Stuttgart.

Racing returns

Work continued on rebuilding Daimler-Benz's production capacity and introducing the new models that would be essential to its survival, but at the same time thoughts were also turning towards re-establishing Mercedes-Benz in motor sport. In 1947 the Daimler-Benz board discussed the idea of producing a sports car and, within six weeks, Rudolf Uhlenhaut had drawn up specific proposals for

how it could be done, developing the idea gradually while the bulk of engineering efforts were going into the development of the 300 saloon and its smaller brother, the 220. Two years later the board made a fundamental decision about the sports car project, allowing it to go ahead but not approving the new engine that Uhlenhaut felt was necessary to achieve his target of 200bhp. Instead he would have to develop an existing Mercedes engine to power the new car and, similarly, much of the running gear for the sports car would have to come from production models.

But Mercedes-Benz's return to motor sport came long before the new sports car was complete. Pre-war racing boss Alfred Neubauer found that some of the 1930s racing cars had survived the war in reasonable condition and, in February 1951, he entered three twelve-year-old W154s in a pair of Formula Libre races in Argentina, the Juan and Eva Peron Grands Prix in Buenos Aires. Local hero José-Froilan Gonzalez – the 'bull of the Pampas' – spoiled Neubauer's party by winning both races in a Ferrari, each time crossing the line ahead of a pair of W154s. Another local lad, Juan Manuel Fangio, put his W154 into pole position for both races, but could finish no better than third as the Mercedes team struggled with tyre and brake problems. Quite why Neubauer felt it necessary for Mercedes-Benz to make this early comeback, with ancient pre-war cars, isn't clear. Perhaps his plan was to demonstrate to the Daimler-Benz board that if reasonable results could be obtained with old cars, excellent results would be within range for a new generation of Mercedes-Benz racing machines – applying some pressure to ensure that the new sports car project got the go-ahead. If that was his aim, then he succeeded.

A few weeks after the April 1951 launch of the 300, the Daimler-Benz board met to consider motor sport plans for the future. Formula 1 was to be the main goal, which meant Uhlenhaut would have to design a new single-seater racing car for a formula that, at that time, called for either a supercharged 1.5-litre engine or an unsupercharged 4.5-litre unit. In the meantime, the sports car project would be given the green light – the objective being to make a mark in sports car racing. Barely a week later *The Motor*'s respected technical editor, Laurence Pomeroy, in his review of the racing sports cars at the Le Mans 24-hour race, noted the presence of some distinguished German spectators during the event. Team manager Alfred Neubauer had travelled to La Sarthe, with drivers Hermann Lang and Karl Kling, and they were accompanied by von Uhrach, technical adviser to Daimler-Benz boss Wilhelm Haspel. The reason for the Germans' visit would soon become clear to everyone.

2 'Sports Light' – The Birth of the SL

At Le Mans, drivers Hermann Lang and Karl Kling and team manager Alfred Neubauer had seen Jaguar's new 3.4-litre XK120C (later known universally as the 'C-type') win by more than 60 miles at an average speed of just over 105mph – but they had also seen two of the three Jaguars expire with mechanical maladies. Clearly, light weight, clever aerodynamics and assured reliability would be essential if

a new Mercedes sports car with a production-based drivetrain was to stand any chance against the established Jaguars, with their much larger and more powerful engines. Late in June 1951, Lang, Kling and Neubauer met with Rudolf Uhlenhaut, Chief Designer Frank Roller and Technical Director Fritz Nallinger to discuss the car's design.

In November 1951 the new sports car,

The Jaguar C-type was an effective blend of bespoke tubular chassis and production-based engine and suspension, which Neubauer and his drivers watched winning at Le Mans in 1951.

known internally as W194, underwent its first tests at the Nürburgring. At this stage there was no bodywork, just a rolling chassis with a seat, revealing that W194 had a new chassis made from dozens of steel tubes. Unlike the tubular frames used by some other manufacturers – which were really just glorified versions of the simple ladder frame – this was a proper 'spaceframe'. It had been carefully designed using stress calculations to determine the precise dimensions and positions required for the chassis tubes, so that they could be as light as possible while still providing the necessary strength and stiffness. Before building the car's chassis, Uhlenhaut's men had made a one-fifth scale model, which they had subjected to bending and torsion (twisting) tests before the chassis design had been signed off.

The full-size finished chassis weighed just 110lb (50kg). The largest open space between the tubes was at the centre, where the driver (and passenger, if a navigator/co-driver was required) would sit and behind them there was a vertical triangulated framework into which the loads from the rear suspension would be fed. A cage of tubes supported the front end of the car, coming together in a distinctive 'peak' at the back of the engine bay. One of the tubes from this peak dived forwards and downwards to the front right corner of the engine bay, over the top of the engine block (which was canted over at 50 degrees to the left) but *under* the exhaust manifold.

Under instruction from the Daimler-Benz board, Uhlenhaut and his team had used the 300 series production car as a starting point for the mechanical components of the new sports car. A high-performance version of the M186 engine, known as M188, had already been developed for use in the 300S two-door cabriolet. Fitted with three downdraught Solex carburettors rather than two, it developed

Spaceframes: Aviation Technology

One of the key factors in the 300SL's speed was its light weight and that derived principally from its spaceframe chassis.

Early cars had been built on simple 'ladder' chassis, constructed from two longitudinal channel-section members with transverse stiffeners at intervals. 'Boxing in' the chassis rails improved stiffness and a further improvement could be obtained by replacing the rails with tubes. But even then these early frames were liable to bend and twist, unless they were very heavily constructed from thick-gauge steel.

For the 300SL Rudolf Uhlenhaut borrowed the spaceframe technique from aircraft design. Instead of relying on two main members, the spaceframe was constructed from a myriad of straight tubes in a triangulated structure. Wherever possible the tubes were positioned so that they were subject to compression loads rather than bending 'moments', as this utilized the properties of the materials in the best possible way. Correctly designed, a spaceframe could be at once very light and very stiff.

But there were drawbacks. The amount of skilled labour required to build a spaceframe was high, so they were expensive and time-consuming to make. Spaceframes were also tricky to turn into practical vehicles, because large open spaces between tubes compromised the structure – and a car needed space for an engine, fuel, a crew and so on.

In Britain, Colin Chapman was introducing spaceframe structures into his Lotus racing cars around the time Mercedes-Benz was using them and many other racing cars would go on to use them in the 1950s and 1960s. The famous 'birdcage' Maserati would emerge with a very visible, and very complex, spaceframe. There's a story that the Maserati chassis was designed by putting a canary inside and welding tubes in the gaps until the canary couldn't escape – but like most good stories, it's highly unlikely.

Eventually, Chapman's use of stressed floor skins in his cars would lead to complete stressed-skin monocoques with no separate chassis frame (again aping aircraft practice), but the spaceframe would continue to be used in other areas of motor racing and for some specialized road cars.

The 300 saloon was popularly called the 'Adenauer Mercedes', as it was a favourite of West German Chancellor Konrad Adenauer. The engine and suspension would form the basis for the 300SL.

The 300S was lighter than the saloon on which it was based and had more power from a more highly tuned engine, but it was still no sports car.

150bhp, 30 per cent more than the saloon engine. For the racing version, designated M194, the compression ratio was increased and a lot of attention given to the shape of the intake and exhaust ports. A tubular exhaust manifold was also fitted, helping raise output to more than 170bhp. For its angled installa-tion in the W194, the engine was given a new cast-alloy sump – at first just a larger version of the 300's wet sump, but a dry-sump system quickly followed, to avoid any problems of starvation as the racing car tackled fast corners. Twin ignition coils were mounted at the back of the engine bay, one as a spare.

Rudolf Uhlenhaut

Born on 15 July 1906 in London, Uhlenhaut had been raised in England and earned a degree in mechanical engineering from the Munich Technical Institute in 1931. That year he had joined Daimler-Benz.

Rudolf Uhlenhaut (left) was the brilliant engineer behind the 300SL and so many other Mercedes-Benz classics.

When Uhlenhaut took charge of Mercedes-Benz racing car design just five years later, he began by looking critically at the existing W25 racing car. Uhlenhaut was a clever and creative engineer, and also a talented driver, and to better understand the feed-back from his drivers he taught himself to drive his own racing cars almost as fast as they could. Not only did the drivers respect him more as a result, but Uhlenhaut now had the capability to find out for himself how Mercedes-Benz cars handled at racing speeds.

The result of his work was the W125, with a heavily revised chassis and up to 646bhp from the supercharged, straight-eight engine displacing 5.7 litres. The W125 put Mercedes-Benz back on top in 1937 but, for 1938, new rules stipulated a maximum engine size of 3.0 litres supercharged or 4.5 litres normally aspirated. Uhlenhaut opted for a new super-charged V12 for the new W154 car, which recorded a 1-2-3 in Tripoli on its debut in 1938 and won cham-pionships for Rudolf Caracciola and Hermann Lang in 1938 and 1939. When the rules for the Tripoli Grand Prix were changed to favour smaller-engined cars – specifically to exclude the Mercedes-Benz and Auto Union teams – Uhlenhaut produced a tiny 1.5-litre V8, the W165. The two cars sent to Tripoli fin-ished first and second.

After the war, Uhlenhaut was appointed head of Daimler-Benz research and development, working on passenger cars and a new generation of racing cars. Following the success of the 300SL sports-racer, Uhlenhaut masterminded a brilliant new Formula 1 car, the W196, for 1954. Technically innovative and beautifully executed, the W196 swept all before it. Juan Manuel Fangio would win two driver's world championships in the car, which would also spawn a sports-racing version, the 300SLR.

Despite his obvious skill as a driver, Uhlenhaut never raced one of his Mercedes-Benz cars: the factory thought too much of him as an engineer to risk him in racing and, in any case, his family com-mitments were too great. But he still attended many races, using his special 300SLR coupé to make rapid journeys across Europe – and demoralizing the oppo-sition by always being in the paddock before anyone else had arrived.

After Daimler-Benz withdrew from racing in 1955 Uhlenhaut concentrated on passenger cars, until his retirement in the 1970s. Even then he was still pushing Mercedes-Benz cars to the limit – it's said his lap time around the Nürburgring Nordschleife was quicker in a 600 Limousine than in a 230SL.

Uhlenhaut died in 1989 at the age of eighty-three, just a few weeks before a new generation of Silver Arrows, Peter Sauber's Mercedes-Benz-powered sports cars, triumphed at Le Mans.

The 300 saloon's independent front suspension was carried over to the SL. Unequal-length upper and lower wishbones tilted each front wheel inwards at the top as the suspension compressed, helping to keep the tyres perpendicular to the road surface (and thus improve grip) when the car rolled in a corner. Coil springs were used, together with telescopic dampers and an anti-roll torsion bar, the damper housings being drilled to lighten them. The inner ends of the wishbones were mounted on a vertical post that was then attached to the chassis, allowing a controlled amount of longitudinal compliance in the suspension: in the saloon it had helped to improve refinement, but a more important benefit for the SL racer was that it would reduce the transmission of road shocks through the steering and help to fight driver fatigue in a big race.

At the front, the 300's suspension had been used with little modification (beyond rudimentary lightening of some components), but the saloon's swing-axle rear suspension was subject to more substantial changes before it found its way into the SL. The coil springs and telescopic dampers were retained, but now moved behind the axles rather than in front as they were on the saloon, and the auxiliary torsion bars fitted to the big saloon were dispensed with. Braking at both ends of the car was by big Al-fin drums (with a finned aluminium shell bonded to a cast-iron inner drum) with twin leading shoes at the front and single leading shoe at the back. The Ferodo VG95 linings were bonded to their shoes rather than riveted.

Further testing at Sindelfingen, the Nürburgring, Hockenheim and even a stretch of autobahn just outside Stuttgart saw the SL in

Despite the heavy production-based engine, the 300SL was light enough to be competitive thanks to a spaceframe chassis welded up from small-diameter tubes. The finished chassis weighed just 110lb (50kg).

Tilting the engine 50 degrees to the right allowed a much lower bonnet line and major improvement in the body's drag coefficient. This ghosted view also clearly shows the 'towers' inboard of the springs, which provided mounting points for the front suspension, and the angled contact face of the cylinder head and block.

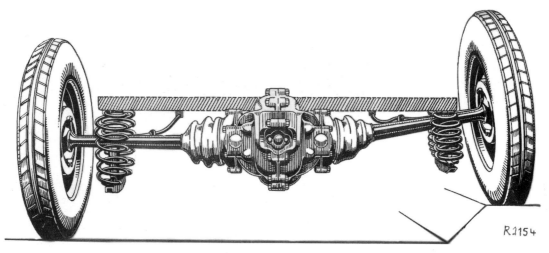

The swing-axle independent rear suspension dated back to the 170 of the 1930s. It offered significant benefits compared to the more common leaf-sprung live axle – but had disadvantages of its own.

the hands of the team's racing drivers and master development driver Uhlenhaut. When the W194 racer was revealed to the press in March 1952, it was painted the now-familiar Mercedes silver and carried a sizable three-pointed star at the front, but there was little else about the car that seemed familiar to the assembled pressmen. Conventional sports racing cars of the time, like the Jaguar C-type, the 4.5-litre Ferrari and the Talbot-Lago, were open roadsters, designed that way to keep weight and frontal area to a minimum. By contrast this new Mercedes was a fixed-roof coupé with a sleek, streamlined appearance – and, apparently, no doors.

The choice of a fixed-roof car had been dictated by the need for ultimate aerodynamic efficiency, so that the W194 could make the most of the comparatively meagre output of its production-based engine. Conventional sports cars were designed with open cockpits to save the weight of a roof and keep frontal area small. By defying convention and opting for a carefully shaped coupé roof on the W194, Mercedes-Benz aimed to trade slightly larger frontal area for a big reduction in drag coefficient and in so doing gain an overall reduction

in drag – not a widely used idea in the 1950s, but by no means a new one. Porsche had built the special low-drag, hard-top VW Type 64 in 1939 and followed that with its own 356 coupés from 1948, while BMW had won the abbreviated 1940 Mille Miglia with a light-weight fixed-roof coupé version of its 328 sports car.

Once the decision had been made to go for a fixed-roof car the team faced two related problems – the first was how to get the driver in and the second was how to meet the regulations, which demanded doors with an opening at least 16in by 8in (406 × 203mm). Jaguar's tube-frame C-type had short doors which extended as far down as they could, until the chassis side members got in the way. On the W194 the chassis tubes at the sides were much higher in the pursuit of structural stiffness, leaving no room in the side of the car for a conventional door of the size required by the regulations.

Gullwing Genius

The solution was as spectacular as it was effective. Rather than extending downwards into

Aerodynamic closed coupés were unusual in the 1950s, but by no means unheard of. BMW had won the shortened Mille Miglia in 1940 with this hard-top 328.

the car's flanks, the W194's doors extended upwards into the roof to produce a reasonably-sized aperture. The doors were hinged near the centre-line of the roof panel, opening upwards and propped open with an over-centre stay. The steering wheel was made easily detachable so that the driver did not have to insinuate his legs around and under it. The only drawback was that the crew had to vault over the high cockpit side to get in – and that competing teams might argue that the Mercedes' doors did not meet the spirit of the regulations. Work was soon under way to revise the chassis side-members, lowering them just enough to allow the doors to extend downwards a little more, so that the opening was a little more like a conventional door shape. This would silence any objections and would also make it easier to get in and out.

The canted-over mounting for the engine had enabled Uhlenhaut and his team to keep the front end of the car low for minimal frontal area. Stylist Karl Wilfert had been responsible for the wind-cheating shape, which had no external seams at all and little decoration except for Mercedes-Benz three-pointed stars on the radiator grille and boot-lid. Even external mirrors were conspicuous by their absence, and the *Tritt zum Einsteigen* – a step in the side of the car to make it easier to climb over the side – had been deleted before the first cars were built, leaving the W194 with a remarkably clean and unfussy shape. Wind-tunnel tests of a one-fifth scale model had forecast a drag coefficient of as little as 0.20, though this climbed to 0.25 for the finished car. Even so, there are still few cars made today that come anywhere near to matching the drag coefficient of the 1950s SL.

Once installed into this low-drag shell, with its narrow 'glasshouse' to minimize frontal area, the driver and navigator found themselves in a cockpit that was comfortable and well-trimmed by racing car standards. Enveloping bucket seats were covered in Mer-cedes' typical plaid cloth and elsewhere there was a mixture of cloth trim and carpet. There were no seat belts. Ahead of the occupants sat a full-width dashboard with a cowled speed-ometer and tachometer taking the prime posi-tion just below the driver's eyeline. Minor instruments – for oil and water temperatures, oil pressure and fuel level – were relegated to the lower part of the dash, where they could be viewed through the bottom half of the steering wheel. A clock with an inset seconds dial was fitted in the centre of the facia, where it could be seen by both driver and navigator. The crew also benefited from excellent heating and ventilation, intended to reduce fatigue during long races.

Light fantastic

The W194's dry weight was around 1,914lb (870kg), 150lb (70kg) more than the original estimates. Of that, nearly 600lb (272kg) was accounted for by the heavy production-based engine and gearbox. The weight reduction achieved by the spaceframe chassis and light-weight aluminium body was remarkable – even the lightest 300S production car weighed over 3,520lb (1,600kg), almost twice as much as the 300SL. But the 300SL was, of course, as big as it needed to be and no bigger: sitting on a 94.5in (2,400mm) wheelbase it was 166in (4,220mm) long and 70.5in (1,790mm) wide – fully 20in (510mm) shorter than the 300S and 4.7in (120mm) narrower.

Neubauer had established that, in race trim, the Ferrari and Jaguar competition weighed around 1,980–2,090lb (900–950kg), so in weight terms the 300SL was competitive, if unremarkable. It also had exceptional aerody-namics and the prospect of good reliability. Would that be enough? Neubauer regarded the car's potential with some scepticism. The Jaguar and Ferrari were much more powerful, he argued, so there was little chance for an overall victory for the new Mercedes-Benz in

Alfred Neubauer

One of the greatest racing team managers of all, Alfred Neubauer's greatest contribution was to bring thoughtful, clear-sighted management to the running of a racing team. The Le Mans victory in 1952 was as much a result of careful planning and organization as it was due to fast cars or skilful drivers.

Alfred Neubauer, the legendary Mercedes racing team manager.

Neubauer was born on 29 March 1891 in a town then known as Neutitsch, in Moravia, part of the Austrian empire (and now known as Novy Jicin, in the Czech Republic). After organizing motor pools and vehicle maintenance during the First World War, Neubauer worked for Austro-Daimler as a test driver and raced Austro-Daimler cars. In 1924 he followed fellow Austrian Ferdinand Porsche to Mercedes and, by 1926, had given up driving to become manager of the racing department.

Neubauer then masterminded the Mercedes–Benz team's rise to glory in the 1930s. It's also said that he unwittingly invented the 'Silver Arrow' nickname. The day before its first race, the W25 – painted white, Germany's national racing colour – turned out to be a kilogram (2lb) over the maximum permitted weight and (so the story goes) driver Manfred von Brauchitsch commented that without a Mercedes in the race the event would be as interesting as watching paint dry. That gave Neubauer the idea to have all the paint scraped and polished off the W25's bodywork – without the paint, it was *just* light enough. The W25 ran in naked aluminium and from then on Mercedes cars were painted silver, just as the rival Auto Unions had always been.

After the Second World War, Neubauer returned to his post at Stuttgart, overseeing first the 300SL sports car effort, and then the W196 Formula 1 and sports cars, both of which would dominate their respective formulas.

Neubauer had a public image as a stern, dictatorial figure and it's true that during races he was very much in charge – and unwilling to accept error or failure. What is less widely known is that in private Neubauer was a jolly man, a bon viveur and a trickster. Stirling Moss recalls an aeroplane flight where the rotund Neubauer joked that his huge frame was stuck in a door. Auto Union driver Bernd Rosemeyer once bet all the drivers they couldn't beat his lap time at Avus, so Neubauer timed Hermann Lang – but clicked his stopwatch early, making Rosemeyer think he had been beaten.

Alfred Neubauer was a hands-on manager: here he lends some extra weight to a pit signal.

But there was also another side to Neubauer, an emotional and understanding side. When Dick Seaman had died racing a Mercedes-Benz in 1939 it had been Neubauer who had spoken at his funeral, moving everyone with an emotional speech. When Neubauer himself died in 1980, motor racing lost not only one of its finest competitors, but also one of its greatest men.

any of the major sports car races. Neubauer put forward the case for a new purpose-designed racing engine, with 200bhp or more to make the car more competitive, and also argued for a five-speed gearbox, the larger-diameter wheels and tyres used on rival cars, and bigger brakes. Uhlenhaut no doubt saw the benefits of all these suggested changes, but pointed out that the factory was already at full stretch with other projects, so the production-based W194 was the best that could be done. Soon they would see if the 300SL was good enough to win.

Racing the W194

The new 300SL made its racing debut in one of the biggest and most demanding sports car

Rudolf Caracciola (left) and Alfred Neubauer had been an almost unbeatable combination in the 1930s. Neubauer recalled Caracciola to Mercedes to drive the 300SL in 1952.

races of all, the Mille Miglia. Back in 1931 Rudolf Caracciola had become the first foreign winner of the 1,000-mile Italian road race in a Mercedes SSKL and the only other non-Italian win had been BMW's 1940 success – though strictly speaking the event had that year been the 'Gran Premio Brescia', not a Mille Miglia, and had been run over nine laps of a very different 103-mile circuit. Whichever way you looked at it, the Mille Miglia had only been won by Italians until the Germans had come along and the Italians had once again dominated the race on the five occasions it had been run since the war, with four wins for Ferrari and one for Alfa Romeo. Now the Germans were back again….

Four 300SLs were sent to Brescia, all now fitted with quick-release hubs and splined wheels in place of the original bolt-on items. One car was a spare and sported the revised door arrangement with the door extending down into the side of the car. This added an extra curved section to the bottom of the door and, with both doors open, the SL reminded onlookers of a gull in flight – to English onlookers, at any rate, who called it a 'Gull-wing' – the French thought of a slightly different type of flight and called it a *papillon* (butterfly), while the Germans called it a *Flügeltürer*, or 'wing door'. The shorter doors on the three race cars quickly became a controversial feature, as the Italian scrutineers initially did not accept them. The Mercedes were only allowed to race after the apertures were measured by Conte Aymo Maggi – the Italian nobleman who was the 'father' of the Mille Miglia – and pronounced legal.

The three race cars were driven by Karl Kling, Hermann Lang and fifty-one-year-old veteran Rudolf Caracciola. Lang and Kling had driven the old W154s during Neubauer's expedition to Argentina a year earlier; Caracciola, the old master, had not raced a car for Daimler-Benz since the Italian Grand Prix in 1939. The circuit used for the Mille Miglia

1952 Racing SL W194

Chassis and body	Tubular steel spaceframe chassis with alloy body panels. Two 'gullwing' doors opening upwards
Engine	Front engine, longitudinal, tilted left at 50 degrees to vertical
Designation	M194
Block material	Cast iron
Head material	Aluminium alloy
Cylinders	6 in-line
Cooling	Water
Lubrication	Dry sump
Bore × stroke	85 × 88mm
Capacity	2996cc
Main bearings	7
Valves/operation	Single chain-driven overhead camshaft, twelve valves operated by finger followers
Compression ratio	8:1
Fuel system	Three Solex downdraught or twin-choke Weber sidedraught carburettors
Maximum power	175bhp at 5,200rpm
Maximum torque	188lb ft
Transmission	Four-speed manual gearbox with synchromesh on all forward ratios. Rear-wheel drive
Gear ratios	3.33–2.12–1.50–1.00 (1-2-3-4)
Clutch	Dry, single-plate
Suspension and steering	
Front	Double wishbones, coil springs, telescopic dampers, anti-roll bar
Rear	Twin-pivot swing axle, coil springs, telescopic dampers
Steering	Recirculating ball
Wheels	Centre-lock steel disc wheels
Tyres	6.70 × 15 cross-ply
Brakes	Hydraulically operated drum brakes all round, with finned light-alloy drums. Air-brake tested in practice at Le Mans
Dimensions	
Length	166in (4,216mm)
Width	70.5in (1,791mm)
Height	49.8in (1,265mm)
Track – front	54.4in (1,382mm)
Track – rear	56.9in (1,445mm)
Wheelbase	94.5in (2,400mm)
Unladen weight	1,914lb (870kg)
Fuel tank capacity	37gal (170ltr)
Performance	
Top speed	150mph (240km/h)
Acceleration	0–62mph (100km/h) approximately 11sec

Caracciola's appearance in the Mille Miglia in 1952 must have brought back memories of his 1931 win in an SSKL – the first time a non-Italian car and driver had won the great race.

had changed a number of times since Caracciola's win: in 1931 the cars had started in Brescia, in the north of Italy, and headed south-west to Piacenza, east to Bologna and then south to Rome. The return leg zig-zagged to the Adriatic coast, back to Bologna, then north to Treviso and east to Brescia. For 1951 the Mille Miglia competitors had lapped Italy clockwise, heading east from Brescia, then following the coast down to Pescara, south-west to Rome, then back to Brescia via Firenza. The route was to be the same in 1952 and would survive until the last Mille Miglia in 1957, but for the addition of a loop to Tazio

Nuvolari's birthplace at Mantua after his death in 1953.

Luigi Villoresi had won the 1951 race in a Ferrari, with Giovanni Bracco twenty minutes adrift in a Lancia Aurelia. For 1952 the fearless Bracco was driving the new Ferrari 250S and quickly took the lead in the rain, chased by the Mercedes trio and Stirling Moss in a Jaguar C-type with the new Dunlop disc brakes. The C-type lost time in a minor accident and Lang retired early after sliding into a stone marker at the side of the road, leaving Kling and Caracciola to chase the Ferrari. Kling overhauled Bracco on the run to Pescara as the Italian

The veteran Caracciola brought his 300SL home fourth in the Mille Miglia, the car's debut event.

Kling battled with Bracco in the Ferrari, but had to settle for second place in the Mille Miglia. A sticking wheel at a pit stop cost him victory.

suffered from tyre wear, but then Bracco fought back from fifth place as other works Ferraris driven by Castellotti and Taruffi retired. While Kling was fortified by hot coffee from the Thermos flasks that had been provided between the SL's front seats, Bracco was taking sips of brandy between cigarettes. Spurring the Ferrari on he caught and passed Kling's Mercedes (which was suffering from brake trouble) and arrived back in Brescia nearly five minutes ahead of the German, with Luigi Fagioli third ahead of Caracciola in the other surviving 300SL. Ferrari had beaten the Mercedes-Benzes, as Neubauer had feared – but it had taken a virtuoso drive from Bracco to achieve it.

The same three drivers reappeared at Berne in May, together with Fritz Riess in a fourth SL, which had acted as spare car at the Mille Miglia. For the Swiss race, Fritz Nallinger had ordered that each car would be a different colour, so that when they arrived in Berne Caracciola's SL was red, Kling's was green and Lang's was blue, with Riess's long-door car still

in its original silver. The main opposition came from a sole works-supported Ferrari, which Willy Daetwyler had put on pole position – happily for Mercedes-Benz it broke its rear axle on the start-line, leaving the 300SLs to take an easy victory. But the Berne race was not an entirely happy one for Mercedes; Kling's green SL may have won with Lang and Riess second and third, but Caracciola had dropped to fourth suffering from brake problems and eventually a rear brake locked and threw him off the road. The SL crashed head-on into a tree, leaving Caracciola with a badly broken leg that would end his long and illustrious racing career.

New for Le Mans

Three new 300SLs were built for the Le Mans 24-hour race in June, all of them with the longer doors seen on Riess's Berne car and fuel fillers sprouting up out of the rear window (where previously the filler had been hidden in the boot). The Le Mans cars also carried twin

---

Track Rivals to the Racing 300SL

The car that in some ways inspired the 300SL and was its natural rival on the track was Jaguar's XK120C ('C' for competition), popularly known as the C-type. The XK120 road car introduced in 1948 had been based on a shortened, lightened version of the Jaguar MkV saloon chassis, but even in alloy-bodied form it was too heavy to compete with purpose-built racing sports cars. The C-type had a much lighter and stiffer steel tube chassis clothed in light-alloy panels and weighed in around 750lb (340kg) lighter than the alloy-bodied XK120, which in turn was about 60lb (27kg) lighter than the steel-bodied production car. Power came from a high-compression version of the XK's 3.4-litre twin-overhead cam engine, developing around 200bhp. At Le Mans in 1951 they were fast in practice and led convincingly until failing oil pressure put two of the cars out before half distance, leaving the third car in the hands of Peter Walker and Peter Whitehead to cruise on to win.

Hurried preparation sidelined the Jaguars in 1952, allowing the 300SLs to win – but not without opposition. The sports-racing Talbot of Pierre Levegh led most of the race and the French marque had already shown its mettle by winning at Le Mans in 1950. Large-capacity American engines powered strong rivals from Nash-Healey, Cunningham and Allard. Ferrari, too, was a contender, but struggled to repeat its victory of 1949 – the extra power of the Aurelio Lampredi-designed 'long block' V12 often took its toll on the Maranello machine's transmissions. As Laurence Pomeroy of *The Motor* remarked, Ferraris went fast, or far – but rarely both.

The battle between the disc-braked 1953 Jaguars and Uhlenhaut's W194, now fuel-injected, would have been a fascinating one. Without the Mercedes challenge the C-type Jaguars were left to record a resounding 1-2, while Stuttgart was already thinking about 1954.

leather bonnet-retaining straps (a peculiarity of the Le Mans regulations) and another new colour scheme: this time the cars were mainly silver, but carried coloured bands around their grilles for identification. Karl Kling shared one of the cars with his Mille Miglia co-driver Hans Klenk, with Lang and Riess in another. With Caracciola out, Theo Helfrich and Helmut Niedermayr were drafted in to drive the third car. Two spare cars were also sent to France for practice, one of them with an enormous pivoted flap mounted on two struts behind the doors. It was an experimental air-brake, which sat horizontally until the driver tipped it forward using a lever in the centre of the cockpit, increasing the SL's frontal area and drag factor to help slow the car from more than 100mph. Already tested on the fast

sweeping bends of Hockenheim, the air brake certainly worked, giving a retardation of about 0.2g at high speed, but concerns over the strength of the mounting struts meant it was left off the cars for the race. It was an idea that would reappear to good effect on the 300SLR of 1955.

Few fancied the Mercedes-Benz cars to do well at Le Mans in 1952, because of the strength of the opposition at the famous French race. Seven Ferraris were headed by the 250S coupé of Alberto Ascari and Luigi Villoresi, and Jaguar were fielding C-types with new low-drag bodywork that had been pressed into service earlier than anticipated after Moss had observed the 300SL's speed during the Mille Miglia. There was a new six-cylinder Gordini for Jean Behra and Robert

Longer doors were quickly evolved to avoid protests. Riess's Berne coupé and the three Le Mans cars all sported the revised door design.

The traditional Le Mans start, with the 300SLs near the middle of the pack. Helfrich (car 20) is already at the door of his car; Lang (21) is still sprinting; while Kling (22) seems to be making a more leisurely start.

Manzon, big Talbots for Meyrat/Mairesse and Levegh/Marchand, and a trio of Chrysler-engined Cunninghams (one with a coupé body). The SLs had mixed fortunes in practice, Lang posting a rapid 4min 40sec lap – a tenth of a second quicker than Ascari in the fastest Ferrari – but the Helfrich/Niedermayr car needed extensive body repairs after a crash. Meanwhile Jaguar struggled with overheating, caused by poor airflow through the radiator on the new long-nose, long-tail C-type.

The cars lined up for the traditional Le Mans start with the 3.0-litre 300SLs in the middle of the pack. Moss made his usual spectacular getaway in one of the Jaguars, but the three SLs were slow to get moving, their drivers taking time to get into the cars and refit the removable steering wheels. After just six laps Ascari's Ferrari was back in the pits for a sixteen minute stop, already showing signs of the clutch failure that would put it out after three hours. By then the Jaguar challenge had collapsed too, all three C-types being forced out with problems caused by the cars' overheating. On Saturday evening Manzon's

Gordini led from Kling in the 300SL, with Helfrich/Niedermayr fifth and Lang/Riess seventh, but then the leading Mercedes slowed, dropping to ninth place before expiring with a broken dynamo at 11.30pm. Ferrari and Cunningham retirements promoted the remaining 300SLs to third and fourth places behind the Gordini and the Talbot-Lago of Pierre Levegh. Then early on Sunday morning the Gordini retired with brake trouble, leaving the Talbot and the two 300SLs ahead of the Lance Macklin/Tommy Wisdom Aston Martin.

Levegh had driven the whole race single handed, while Neubauer was sticking to his plan of running the SLs at a reliable pace rather than risk a failure by chasing the Frenchman. Further time was being lost to the French car because tyre wear had proved to be greater than the engineers had anticipated, necessitating more frequent wheel changes (as Neubauer had feared). The Talbot lasted until just seventy-two minutes from the end, when a connecting rod bearing failed – perhaps due to an error by Levegh, by now exhausted and

The Kling/Klenk 300SL chases the sister car of Helfrich/Niedermayr just after the start of another Le Mans lap. The inexperienced Helfrich and Niedermayr would bring their car home in second place.

Kling and Klenk led the 300SL charge at Le Mans until their car retired with dynamo failure just before midnight.

driving without a working rev-counter. That left the Lang/Riess 300SL to sweep by into the lead and go on to an easy victory, covering 2,320 miles (3,733km) in the twenty-four hours at an average of 96.7mph (155.6km/h), with the Helfrich/Niedermayr car a lap behind (they had been delayed by a damaged wheel, which had enforced a slow return to the pits for repairs) to claim a 1-2 for Mercedes-Benz. The French crowd, denied a dramatic home win, greeted the Gullwings with polite applause.

37

The Lang/Riess 300SL heads out away from the Esses. After Levegh's Talbot expired, the pair would inherit the win.

Four roadster 300SLs were entered for the Nürburgring sports car race in August 1952. Lighter weight was deemed more important than ultimate aerodynamic efficiency.

Home Win

The sports car race supporting the German GP at the Nürburgring in August attracted a relatively sparse entry, with only a Gordini and a single semi-works Ferrari to challenge a Mercedes-Benz team that was there in force for its home race. No less than six 300SLs were present, two coupés and four cars in a new roadster form – three of them converted from coupé specification and a fourth built up from scratch with a wheelbase 8in (200mm) shorter than standard and a narrower air-intake grille at the front. The thinking was that, on the tortuous Nürburgring, light weight and good visibility were more important than high-speed aerodynamic efficiency and, to ensure that the roadsters were as light as possible, the interiors were simplified – even to the extent of minimizing the instrumentation. Yet another colour scheme adorned the cars, which were again predominantly silver, but this time sported coloured flashes above and below the headlights for identification. A supercharged

engine with a gear-driven Roots-type blower was tried in practice, but the unblown engine's reliability was chosen ahead of the blown engine's 230bhp power output. It was an easy victory for Mercedes-Benz, Lang heading a 1-2-3-4 win in his now roofless ex-Le Mans car after early leader Kling in the short-wheelbase car suffered from oil leaking into the cockpit.

A tougher challenge awaited at the Carrera Panamericana, a 2,000-mile road race across Mexico that had been inaugurated in 1950 to celebrate completion of the Mexican stretch of the Pan-American Highway. The Carrera was reckoned by many to be harder on car and driver than any of the European road races, including the classic Targa Florio, Mille Miglia and Vingt-Quatre Heures du Mans – but the Mercedes had already proved more reliable than any of its rivals and the company's South American distributor urged them to take part. So, in September, four 300SLs were shipped to Mexico: Karl Kling had his Le Mans coupé, there was a brand new coupé for Hermann Lang, a roadster for a new signing, the American John Fitch (who had impressed everyone driving for Cunningham at Le Mans earlier in the year) and another roadster as a spare, which was driven from stage to stage by Neubauer's assistant, journalist Günther Molter. Kling was with his regular co-driver Hans Klenk, while Lang was back with his Mille Miglia navigator Erwin Grupp and Fitch was partnered by mechanic Eugen Geiger.

Kling's short-wheelbase roadster (with its slightly narrower grille) leads in the early stages at the Nürburgring. Competition for the 300SLs was sparse.

Lang won the Nürburgring race in his long-wheelbase roadster.

Two roadsters were modified for the Carrera Panamericana, with full-width windscreens and a seat for the co-driver.

The cars retained their Nürburgring colour schemes, but a number of other changes were made for the Carrera. The two roadsters (both long-wheelbase cars) were given passenger seats and full-width windscreens in place of their original driver-only aeroscreens, while the lanky Fitch was given an extra windscreen mounted on stalks above the main screen. The coupés reverted to a fuel filler in the boot instead of the Le Mans-type filler emerging from the rear window (because fast refuelling stops were not thought important for the Carrera) and gained bright chrome trim around their windows. In earlier races the exhaust pipe had been run between the chassis tubes on the passenger side of the car, but now it exited through the side of the car below the passenger door, which must have made it a noisy race for Geiger in the roadster's passenger seat. Single leather bonnet-straps were fitted, unlike the double straps required at Le Mans. As there was no '3.0-litre' class in the Carrera, all four cars had their engines bored out from 85mm to 86.5mm to increase the engine capacity to 3,103cc, developing 177bhp at 5,200rpm.

Trouble Strikes

The SLs hit trouble almost straight away. Barely had the cars left the start at Tuxtla Guttierez when Lang hit a dog at speed, rearranging the front of his coupé. All three race cars quickly hit tyre problems, because Continental, who as usual were supplying the tyres for the SLs, had not had time to analyse the road conditions, as the decision to compete in the Carrera had come too late. The tyres they had supplied were the same as those used at the Nürburgring and on the fast Mexican roads they overheated and threw treads. As a result all three cars had to stop during the first stage to change tyres – not once but *three* times. And worse was to come.

As the Kling/Klenk coupé streaked north towards Oaxaca at around 140mph (225km/h), the 300SL collided with a flying buzzard, which smashed straight through the laminated windscreen and into Klenk's face. Klenk was

The Mercedes team in Mexico. From left: Grupp and Lang, Klenk and Kling, and the roadster of Fitch and Geiger.

Lanky American John Fitch (left) had impressed Neubauer with his drive for Cunningham at Le Mans earlier in the year. He joined the Mercedes team for the Carrera.

Pandemonium as the Kling/Klenk SL makes a stop after a buzzard had smashed through the (laminated) windscreen. While a bloodied Klenk emerges and Neubauer demands all the details, Kling coolly lights a cigarette.

Fitch in the roadster, before an extra screen was fitted for him above the main windscreen.

Tyre stop for the battered Kling/Klenk 300SL: note the damaged windscreen.

dazed, but amazingly suffered no serious injury, so the pair continued – Klenk wearing goggles until the windscreen could be replaced. At that point the crew also elected to fit 'buzzard bars' over the windscreen, to protect them from any other wildlife that might underestimate the

speed of the Mercedes. Klenk later found that, as a result of his encounter with the bird, he had been given the nickname *Geier*, German for 'vulture'.

Ferrari provided the main threat to the 300SLs, as always, but once again the speed of the machines from Maranello was not matched by their reliability. Giovanni Bracco fought for the lead with his Mille Miglia adversary Kling until he succumbed to axle

41

About to get going again after a tyre stop, Kling dons his racing helmet while Klenk (already wearing goggles) tidies up.

Kling sits on the door sill at a pit stop, the 300SL now wearing the 'buzzard bars' fitted after the accident.

Karl Kling, relaxing with cigarette in hand, and co-driver Hans Klenk got their own back on Mille Miglia winner Bracco in the Carrera.

failure, leaving the 300SL to claim victory in the Carrera Panamericana at record pace after a stunning drive from Kling, with Lang and Grupp in second place. Fitch was absent from the results, disqualified on a technicality after reversing into a service area for attention to deranged steering, but after representations from Neubauer to the organizers he was allowed to complete the course and even picked up an award for the fastest time on the final leg.

The SLs ended 1952 with an enviable record: five races, with four wins and five second places. From a total of seventeen entries the W194s had failed to finish just three times, all of which proved that the new Mercedes was both reliable and swift enough to challenge the best sports racing cars Britain, Italy and France could pit against it. Ferrari, in particular, was ready to take on the might of Mercedes in sports car racing and all eyes turned towards 1953.

Kling produced one of the finest drives of his career to win the Carrera Panamericana.

'Buzzard bars' over the windscreen should be unique to the Kling/Klenk Carrera Panamericana 300SL – though a replica was later built for show.

The definitive 'long-door' 300SL shape, some elements of which would remain in the production 300SL road car.

3 Gullwing –
The SL Becomes a Road Car

By the end of 1952 Rudolf Uhlenhaut was already planning major improvements to the W194 racing car for the new season. Chassis number 11, known inside Mercedes as the *Hobel* ('old banger'), was built-up early in 1953 with improvements to almost every area – the chassis was revised, the bodywork was very different, the engine had been given a radical new fuel system and the running gear had been modified. The new car promised to be even quicker and better handling than the 1952 racers had been, still more reliable and even more competitive.

The new car was slightly smaller than the W194, built on a 90.6in (2,300mm) wheelbase that was mid-way between the original 300SL coupé and the short-chassis roadster that had been built for the Nürburgring sports car race. *Hobel* was also slimmer, with front and rear tracks about 3in (76mm) narrower, the combined effect being to reduce overall weight by about 143lb (65kg).

Hobel looked a lot different too, with new aerodynamic ideas that had been tested, as before, in one-fifth scale form. The gullwing doors remained, but the simple ventilation flap that had been fitted at the back of the roof on the racing cars had now become a properly-shaped vent and there were many other departures from the W194's styling in the pursuit of still greater aerodynamic efficiency. New thinking about the management of air into and

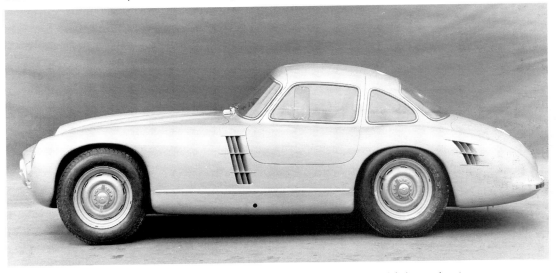

Hobel or 'old banger' was the prototype for the 1953 racing SL, with a shorter wheelbase and fuel-injected engine.

When the 1953 sports car racing programme was abandoned, Hobel *became the prototype for a road-going SL.*

out of the car led to a bigger, squarer air-intake at the front and air-exit vents in the front wings, behind the wheels. These helped to remove hot air from the engine bay, to keep underbonnet temperatures down, and reduced drag by ensuring that air entering at the front of the engine bay had an easy exit path. Small brake-cooling vents were added in the rear wings, the tail itself being longer and sleeker than the original 300SL's rather dumpy rump. Further efforts had been made to lower the bonnet line, which was now so low that a streamlined bulge had to be added on one side so that it would clear the highest point on the engine. Karl Wilfert's styling team added a corresponding bulge on the other side of the bonnet to even up the appearance.

Underneath the bonnet, the engine had also been the subject of considerable development but the source of the new technology the engine employed was an unexpected one – to those outside Daimler-Benz, at least. Benz had been building diesel engines before the Daimler and Benz merger in 1926 and Mercedes-Benz had introduced the world's first diesel passenger car, the 260D, in 1936. At

the same time they had been experimenting with the use of diesel-type direct fuel-injection equipment on petrol engines, both in motor racing and on the DB600 aero-engine that went into the Messerschmitt Bf 109 fighter plane during the war. Now they applied similar technology to the 300SL's M194 engine.

A conventional low-pressure pump supplied fuel to a Bosch mechanical injection pump mounted on the left-hand side of the block, which almost looked like a scale model of the engine itself; a shaft from the engine's timing gears at the front of the block drove a tiny camshaft inside the pump, which in turn operated six vertical plungers, each of which pumped fuel directly into one of the combustion chambers through one of six fuel injectors fitted in the cylinder walls where the spark plugs had been. The plugs were now relocated into deep pockets in the cylinder head, which meant they were a little easier to get to, though still buried under the inclined engine. The revised head also included larger valves for more power. There was a new intake manifold feeding air to the cylinders through six long curved inlet-tracts, which were all supplied from a common cylindrical plenum chamber picking up cold air from a scoop next to the radiator header-tank at the front of the engine bay. The 17in-long intake runners encouraged resonant effects, which improved cylinder filling in the upper half of the engine's speed range – effectively a mild, but free, supercharge, one which had not been possible with the old carburettor installation because there was no space for long enough intakes. The throttle plate was positioned at the head of the plenum chamber, and the accelerator pedal was linked to both the throttle and a mechanism that bled fuel away from the injector pump at small throttle openings, giving precise control of the air/fuel ratio in the cylinders. The system also incorporated automatic compensation for air temperature and density, but not for cold starting: a manually-operated 'choke' control was still provided for cold-start enrichment.

One of the benefits of the system was that the air in the cylinders was cooled by the

Left-hand side of the engine shows the fuel injection pump, with injectors using the old spark-plug locations in the side of the block.

Fuel Injection

Before the W198, all cars had carburettors to control the air/fuel mixture entering the engine. Air flowing into the engine passed through a constriction or 'venturi', which caused the pressure of the air to drop momentarily. A fuel pipe could be placed in the wall of the venturi and the lower pressure of the incoming air would suck fuel out of the pipe. The fuel would then mix with the air as the mixture travelled through the carburettor and down to the cylinder, hopefully creating a uniform air/fuel mixture.

But the venturi or 'choke' that is essential to the carburettor's operation causes a restriction which saps power. A wide venturi is necessary if the engine is to ingest enough air to produce a high power output, but big chokes mean low gas speeds at low revs, which results in poor mixing of the fuel and air and consequent rough running at low revs. A carburettor needs compensating systems for idling, slow running and acceleration, or it will fail to deliver the right air/fuel ratio in each condition. In fact, one wag once defined a carburettor as an instrument scientifically designed to supply the wrong air/fuel mixture at all times.

With fuel injection there is no need for the restrictive venturi and the amount of fuel entering the cylinders can be precisely metered under all conditions, both of which can help extract more power from the engine. As injection systems progressed it was found that there were benefits for exhaust emissions and fuel economy, and the driver's life was made easier with sophisticated mechanical, and then electronic, control systems for cold starts.

Mercedes-Benz used fuel injection (injecting into the manifold rather than the cylinders) on its top models from the mid-1950s onwards, and other marques (notably Maserati and Triumph) introduced it in the 1960s. But widespread adoption of fuel injection did not come until the introduction by Bosch of much lower-priced mechanical injection equipment in the 1970s. Today, all cars use fuel injection – now controlled by electronics.

injection of fuel, reducing any potential for pinking. Effectively the octane rating of the fuel was increased, which meant that the compression ratio could be safely raised from the 8.0:1 of the W194s to 8.6:1. The engine capacity remained at 2996cc (to stay within the 3.0-litre racing class) and, in this form, the power output of what was now known as the M198 engine jumped to 214bhp at 5,960rpm – up more than 20 per cent from the best output seen on carburettors. Flexibility was also vastly improved by the fuel injection system, allowing the SL to pull convincingly from under 18mph (30km/h) to more than 155mph (250km/h) in top gear.

During 1952 the W194's tyres and brakes had come in for considerable criticism and *Hobel*'s design sought to make improvements in these two critical areas. Better brake cooling had been planned in and the car now used the 16in wheels and tyres that Alfred Neubauer had wanted right from the start – on the 15in tyres used in 1952 tyre wear had been dramatic

at Le Mans and almost catastrophic on the Carrera Panamericana. The bigger wheels also made room for even bigger brake drums, though there was as yet no move to fit Jaguar-style disc brakes. Other running gear revisions included moving the gearbox to the back of the car for improved weight distribution and fitting a new form of swing-axle rear suspension with a common fulcrum for the half axles under the final-drive casing. Both the 'low pivot' suspension and the rear-mounted gearbox would also be features of the all-conquering W196 Grand Prix car, and later the 300SLR sports car.

Changing Priorities

After promising tests at the Solitude circuit near Stuttgart early in 1953, Daimler-Benz laid plans to make ten replicas of the new racing coupé, five of them to be ready for the start of the sports car season at the Mille Miglia in April. But, if anything, the fact that Ferrari had challenged Mercedes to a sports car duel in 1953 proved that the W194 had already said everything Mercedes needed to say about its sports cars: they had beaten the top teams, Ferrari and Jaguar, had won everything worth winning – Mille Miglia apart – and had little left to prove. On top of that, it was clear that moving into Grand Prix racing, which had always been the long-term goal, was going to require long and careful development of an advanced racing car, which would take all the racing department's resources. So Mercedes' competition priorities switched to Grand Prix racing with the W196 and the 300SL racing cars were retired. Ferrari, convinced that his cars could have beaten the Mercedes in 1953, was incensed.

But that was far from the end for the 300SL. In 1952 Max Hoffman had been appointed as the distributor for Mercedes-Benz cars on the East Coast of the USA and, following the 300SL's successes in Europe and, in particular, in the Carrera Panamericana in Mexico, Hoffman felt that a production version of the car would sell well. Legend has it that he not only told Daimler-Benz management that he could sell a thousand road-going 300SLs in America, he backed up his claim with a down-payment on them all.

That September, Hoffman surprised the crowds at a sports car race meeting at Bridgehampton, on Long Island, by turning up in one of the 1952 300SL racing coupés. It was the car Karl Kling had used to finish second in the Mille Miglia and then win at Berne in May the previous year, which had been repainted from the green livery it had used in the Swiss race to a more Mercedes-like silver. The brightwork around the windows, which the coupés had sported in the Carrera Panamericana, had also been fitted, but the car had not been given the side-exit exhaust used on the Carrera cars. Though not competing, the 300SL naturally caused something of a stir: was Hoffman generating a little curiosity and publicity because he knew what was just around the corner?

A 300SL Road Car

Uhlenhaut and his team had spent 1953 developing the 300SL, not into an even more

---

Max Hoffman

New York-based Austrian émigré Max Hoffman had made his name selling European sports cars in America. After the war, returning American servicemen had brought with them an enthusiasm for the taut, nimble sports cars epitomized by MG and sales of these cars in the USA had boomed in the late 1940s. Hoffman had been instrumental in the success of Jaguar's XK120 in the USA and had gone on to sell the first Porsche-badged road car, the 356, in some numbers. He also introduced many Americans to BMW and Alfa Romeo cars.

But Hoffman was far more than just a dealer. In tune with his market, he regularly badgered the car makers whose products he sold to make changes or introduce new models. He was behind the introduction of the low-priced, lightweight Porsche 356 Speedster and had encouraged American-domiciled Count Albrecht Goertz to meet with BMW to discuss a new roadster, which became the 507. And, of course, it was Hoffman's enthusiasm that helped the 300SL Gullwing into production, along with the 190SL and 300SL roadsters. By then Hoffman's involvement with Mercedes-Benz was coming to an end, as the Stuttgart company sought to create a North American subsidiary to handle its own distribution of cars in the USA.

Not everything he tried was a success: there was a brief flirtation with Volkswagens in the early fifties, for instance, which came to little. But Hoffman's vision and drive were certainly important factors in the creation of some of the most fondly-remembered sports cars of the era.

formidable racing car, but into the road-going machine that Max Hoffman had been so keen to put on sale. The market it was aimed at was made clear by the venue for its debut – the International Motor Sports Show in New York, in January 1954, where it stole the show. Its styling was, if anything, even more dramatic than that of the W194 and under the skin it had technology that surpassed that of the racing cars on which it was based. It was a fully fledged road car with more power than the 1952 Le Mans winner, yet docile enough to drive on the roads every day and without the reliability worries that blighted some Italian and British sports cars.

The car displayed at New York was based heavily on Uhlenhaut's prototype 1953 racing car, *Hobel*, but much had changed between the decision not to build it as a racing car for 1953 and the unveiling of a road-going production version in 1954. Unlike the short-wheelbase *Hobel*, the production 300SL – known internally as W198 – had reverted to the longer 94.5in (2,400mm) wheelbase of the original racing coupés and at 178in (4,520mm) overall it had grown by a foot compared to the racers. *Hobel* had been made shorter so it could be lighter than the 1952 racing machines, but the longer production car was much heavier. At 2,855lb (1,295kg) fuelled and roadworthy, it tipped the scales around 430lb (195kg) heavier than its racing cousins. Even so, it was still something of a lightweight compared to its road-car rivals: while the expensive Ferrari 250GT with its tubular frame and aluminium-alloy body weighed much the same, the steel-bodied Jaguar XK120 and glassfibre Chevrolet Corvette were up to 100lb (45kg) or so heavier, and both had soft tops.

Much of the increase in weight over the W194 was accounted for by the production car's predominantly steel body, in place of the all-aluminium shell used on the racers. The bonnet and boot lid were still aluminium, however, as were the doors – which otherwise would have been too heavy to comfortably lift. The racing cars had been fitted with simple over-centre folding props to keep the doors open and a simple sliding-bolt extending into the B-pillar to keep them closed. On both short- and long-door cars the door handles were simple half-turn levers at the bottom of the windows. The road car was a little more sophisticated: a pair of hydraulic struts was fitted to help hold the doors up once they were open, and a proper latch and lock were inserted into door, mating with a striker in the sill. The door handles were almost flush fitting,

The road car carried over the racer's spaceframe chassis, but added a new fuel-injected engine.

The road-going 300SL was the star of the International Motor Sports Show at New York in January 1954. Note the prototype 190SL and new 180 Ponton *saloon beyond.*

the New York show car being provided with finger recesses above the handles. On production cars only a tiny thumb-button broke the smooth lines of the door; pressing the button caused the main lever to pop out for use.

Winding windows were not part of the car's specification, however, because the curved door provided nowhere for the window glass to drop down into. Instead the windows were removable, and could be stowed behind the seats in a protective bag. Conventional opening quarter-lights were provided for ventilation.

Revisions for the Road

W198 took the styling ideas that had first been seen on *Hobel* and developed them still further. The larger, squarer air-intake at the front was now a smoother, softer shape but it retained the huge Mercedes-Benz star that had been a feature of the racing 300SLs and the bold chrome bar that had appeared on the prototype. The bonnet still had its twin bulges and it was hinged at the front, as on *Hobel*, rather than at the back, as it had been on the racers. But where *Hobel*'s bonnet had extended all the way to the air intake, the W198's stopped

1954–57 'Gullwing' 300SL W198

Chassis and body	Tubular steel spaceframe chassis with steel body panels (factory code 198.040) or light-alloy panels (198.043). Two 'gullwing' doors opening upwards
Engine	Front engine, longitudinal, tilted left at 45 degrees to vertical
Designation	M198 I
Block material	Cast iron
Head material	Aluminium alloy
Cylinders	6 in-line
Cooling	Water
Lubrication	Dry sump
Bore × stroke	85 × 88mm
Capacity	2996cc
Main bearings	7
Valves/operation	Single chain-driven overhead camshaft, twelve valves operated by finger followers
Compression ratio	8.55:1
Fuel system	Direct fuel injection, mechanically controlled, Bosch 6-plunger pump
Maximum power	215bhp at 5,800rpm
Maximum torque	203lb ft at 4,600rpm
Transmission	Four-speed manual gearbox with synchromesh on all forward ratios. Rear-wheel drive
Gear ratios (1-2-3-4-R)	3.34–1.97–1.39–1.00–2.73
Clutch	Dry single-plate
Final-drive ratio	3.64, 3.25, 3.42, 3.89 or 4.11
Suspension and steering	
Front	Double wishbones, coil springs, telescopic dampers, anti-roll bar
Rear	Twin-pivot swing axle, coil springs, telescopic dampers
Steering	Recirculating ball
Wheels	5K × 15 centre-lock steel disc wheels
Tyres	6.50-15 cross-ply
Brakes	Hydraulically operated drum brakes all round, with finned light-alloy drums
Dimensions	
Length	178in (4,521mm)
Width	70.5in (1,790mm)
Height	51.2in (1,300mm)
Track – front	54.5in (1,384mm)
Track – rear	56.5in (1,435mm)
Wheelbase	94.5in (2,400mm)
Unladen weight	2,849lb (1,295kg)
Fuel tank capacity	22gal (100ltr)
Performance	
Top speed	up to 161mph (260km/h) depending on axle ratio
Acceleration	0–100km/h approximately 10sec

short, leaving a fixed slam-panel at the nose – like the original W194 coupés. The most striking additions to the road car were the 'eyebrows' above the wheel arches at all four corners, which served to break up the otherwise slab-sided shape. Daimler-Benz also claimed that they had an aerodynamic function, separating the airflow over the top of the car from that around the sides, helping to keep the windows clean in bad weather.

Naturally enough, the racing cars had been about function rather than style, so they lacked much external embellishment, giving them a rather austere appearance. New external brightwork lifted the appearance of the road-going 300SL, as far as mid-1950s tastes were concerned, though compared to some cars at the time (particularly in the USA) the use of chrome trim was restrained, to say the least.

The headlight surrounds were now plated, there was a bright air-intake grille at the base of the windscreen and a bright strip along the lower part of the body between the wheels to lower the car visually. The vents in the front wings were wider than those on *Hobel* and now carried twin horizontal chrome trim-strips, while the rear wing vents had been deleted altogether.

Another change that was dropped on the production 300SL was the low-pivot swing-axle, which Daimler-Benz clearly did not yet think was ready for a production car – even a comparatively low-volume one like the 300SL. Instead, the coupé made do with the original racing SL swing-axle layout, which was, of course, closely related to that in the 300 saloon. The brakes, too, were still the racing car's huge drums, when it might have

A characteristic pose, with those instantly-recognizable doors open. The knock-off wheels and leather trim were optional.

been expected that Daimler-Benz would take advantage of the new disc brake technology that was by then available. But arguably there was no need: the aluminium-finned drum brakes on the SL were highly developed and effective.

Inside the 300SL

For a racing car the original 300SL had been well-appointed inside, but the road car was, naturally, trimmed and equipped to an even higher standard. Wider, flatter seats were fitted, with the accent on comfort rather than retention of the body in fast corners, the driver's seat being adjustable fore and aft. Like all the Mercedes racing cars of the era, tartan cloth was the standard trim material, but the 300SL also came with the option of luxurious leather. There was full carpeting, with vinyl trim panels covering the prominent sills and the inside of the doors. The instrument layout was very similar to the racer, with two large main dials and four subsidiary gauges in pairs either side of the steering column, but, in addition, there was also a row of controls scattered across the dash. These included the heating and ventilation levers, controls for cold-start enrichment and a hot-start auxiliary electric fuel pump, and even a duplicate horn button for the passenger, all contained in a thick chrome strip that ran the width of the dashboard. The steering wheel was a typical Mercedes road-car wheel, made of white plastic and large in diameter. Unlike the racing car wheel, which was removable for easier entry and exit, the road car's could be tilted back at the top until it was almost horizontal. Behind the seats there was a semi-circular, carpeted shelf, which was the only real luggage space in the car – the boot was almost useless for carrying luggage because it was full of spare wheel and fuel filler, as the W194's bigger boot area had been sacrificed in favour of a more aerodynamic tail shape. Underneath, behind

the fuel tank, sat a large transverse silencer to reduce exhaust noise, which meant that the road car's tailpipe was on the left of the car rather than the right.

Rapturous Reception

Almost inevitably the press were bowled over by the new Mercedes. In Britain, Gregor Grant's fledgling motor sport magazine *Autosport* described the SL as 'a car with a wonderful external appearance, coupled with virtually unbelievable performance', while German car magazine *auto, motor und sport* said it was 'the most refined and the most fascinating' of all sports cars. In the USA, *Road & Track* explained that the 300SL's combination of refined comfort, remarkable handling and grip, precise steering and breathtaking performance meant just one thing: 'the sports car of the future has become reality.' British journalists got a chance to experience the 300SL in October 1954, when Rudolf Uhlenhaut demonstrated one of the cars at Silverstone just prior to the London Motor Show in 1954, and all were impressed by both the car and by Uhlenhaut's mastery behind the wheel.

But few people actually had the opportunity of driving the car for some time after the launch. Production began slowly, with just 146 cars coming off the line during 1954, rising to a peak of 867 in 1955 and then falling back to 300 in 1956 and 76 in 1957, the year production ended. Essentially, the 300SL was hand-built, as it had to be given its spaceframe chassis, which had been designed for light weight and stiffness in service, not ease of manufacture.

Shortly after production began, the long angled gearlever that had seen service on the racing coupés was swapped for a short remote-change item between the seats. That was just about the only important production change that occurred during the Gullwing's production run, though there were a few options

For road-car customers the interior was made slightly more civilized with better trim. The steering wheel was now tiltable rather than removable.

Doors closed, the 300SL road car offered a smooth, efficient silhouette.

For a show-stopping entrance, it was difficult to beat a Gullwing 300SL.

Max Hoffman is said to have told Daimler-Benz that he could sell 1,000 Gullwings in America: production quickly exceeded that figure.

available that could skew the SL's specification towards the luxury end or the performance end, depending on the customer's requirements. For the sybaritic, leather upholstery could be specified to replace the standard cloth and to make the best use of the limited luggage space Mercedes offered a pair of fitted suitcases with retaining straps – very rarely seen today and a collectors' item in their own right. For the few who raced 300SLs (and the greater number who merely wanted a faster road car) there was the choice of a 'competition' camshaft with more aggressive valve timing to squeeze a few more horsepower from the engine. Mercedes-Benz claimed that the car would reach around 150mph (240km/h) with the standard (3.64:1) axle, and there were two longer final-drives to choose from – 3.42:1, good for 155mph (248km/h), and 3.25:1, on which the SL could top 160mph (256km/h). Like the racing W194, the W198 used steel wheels with aluminium-alloy rims, and these were commonly fitted with specially developed Continental 6.70×15 cross-ply tyres, but the standard bolt-on wheels could be replaced with quick release wheels and Rudge splined-hubs, with two-eared knock-off nuts. Racing tyres like Dunlop's Extra Super Sport – still a cross-ply design, of course – were often fitted. Later an aluminium body was made available, shaving about 200lb (91kg) from the SL's overall weight, though only twenty-nine of these lightweight cars were built.

The low angle of this shot emphasizes the twin bulges in the bonnet. Only the right-hand bulge was needed, to clear the injection plenum, the left-hand bulge simply evening up the appearance.

Racing Certainty

Though the W198 had been built as a road car and had been modified from its racing beginnings to make it more acceptable as everyday transport, it was almost a foregone conclusion that it would find its way into competition – despite its king's ransom price tag of DM29,000 or nearly $7,000 in 1954. By the mid-fifties there was a growing interest in racing categories for production sports or 'Grand Touring' (GT) cars, which often produced close racing and often seemed more relevant to the man in the street, because the cars were ostensibly road-legal machines. Porsche and Lotus were notable performers amongst the smaller-engined production sports cars, while bigger-capacity classes attracted cars from Ferrari, Jaguar and Aston Martin. It was here that the 300SL made its mark.

The Mille Miglia of 1955 was one example. It provided a famous win for Stirling Moss and Denis Jenkinson in a Mercedes 300SLR, 'Jenks' reading pace-notes from a specially-constructed box containing a long roll of paper that he wound from one roller to another. Informed of road hazards using a system of sign language, Moss knew exactly when he could keep his foot down and exploited the system to put up a record 98mph (157km/h) average speed, winning by

more than half an hour from Fangio in a second 300SLR. Meanwhile John Fitch, the American who had joined the 1952 300SL team at the Carrera Panamericana, partnered Belgian driver Olivier Gendebien to a GT-class win in a 300SL, and there were two more SLs taking the second and third places in the class.

Gendebien recorded another fine result in the 300SL that year by winning the tough Liège–Rome–Liège rally, a performance that led to him being offered a works Ferrari sports car drive in 1956 (and subsequently a glittering sports car career, which included four Le Mans wins). Another Belgian, 'Wild' Willy Mairesse, took a 300SL to a fine third at the GT race supporting the German Grand Prix in 1956 and gave the SL a second successive 'Liège' win, a victory that brought him to the attention of the Equipe Nationale Belge sports car racing team. Werner Engel won the European rally championship in 1955 in a pre-production SL, though sadly he would be killed a couple of years later at the wheel of a 300SL Roadster. Walter Schock and his co-driver Rolf Moll won the European championship in 1956, using a 300SL for part of the season. Meanwhile, Paul O'Shea won the Sports Car Club of America's production sports car championship in 1955 and 1956.

The longer tail of the road car aided aerodynamics and allowed for a slightly larger boot.

Uhlenhaut's 'Competition Coupé'

Mercedes-Benz returned to sports car racing in 1955 with the 300SLR, a new racing car based on its championship-winning W196 Grand Prix car. That same year Rudolf Uhlenhaut turned up at races in a road car that seemed to be a 300SL Gullwing – but was in fact a very different car. The 'Competition Coupé', as it was known, was nothing less than a road-legal hard-top version of the full-race 300SLR roadster.

The 'Competition Coupé' looked much like an SL, but featured straight-eight power from the 300SLR.

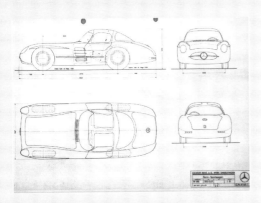

Lower and sleeker than the 300SL, Uhlenhaut's Competition Coupé was one of the fastest road cars of the fifties.

Two of these very special cars were built, based around the 300SLR spaceframe and fitted with its 3.0-litre, 310bhp M196/100 engine. Under the bonnet there were clear differences between this and the 300SL: the engine was tilted over to the right, as in the SLR rather than the left as in the SL, and hidden underneath were sixteen spark plugs, two for each of eight cylinders. From outside the Coupé

Uhlenhaut in the Competition Coupé, about to take his son Roger for a ride.

looked much like a 300SL, but the side-exit exhaust, 300SLR-style nose with cowls over the headlamps and racing wire-spoke wheels gave the game away. Parked next to a 300SL the Competition Coupé was clearly much lower and sleeker than the production car, with a smaller glass area, a more rounded roofline and shorter doors.

Though it was a substantial 476lb (216kg) heavier than the racing SLR thanks to the roof, doors and extra glass, the Competition Coupé was just about the fastest car on the road anywhere in the world in 1955. A top speed in excess of 175mph (280km/h) was recorded, and the 0–60mph sprint took just 6.8 seconds. It was also one of the noisiest cars around, thanks to those fat exhaust pipes that terminated ahead of the passenger door. The car was used as a research tool and allowed Uhlenhaut to display his driving prowess to journalists – and, sometimes, his son Roger.

Uhlenhaut delighted in turning up at European Grand Prix races well ahead of the main Mercedes party and before all the other teams, so that the first thing competitors saw on arrival was his gleaming silver Mercedes supercar parked in the paddock. Like as not the W196 would then go on to dominate the race.

Mercedes-Benz's rapid racing car transporter, here carrying a W196 Formula One car, was powered by a 300SL engine.

The Gullwing SL's competition successes merely added to the mystique of the car, a blue-blooded racing machine that had the refinement expected of a road car, unmatched flexibility and the reliability of a Mercedes. It had dramatic styling that almost nothing could equal and in America the Chevrolet Corvette's stylists stopped trying to make their car look like a Jaguar XK120 and started aping the SL, adding twin bonnet bulges and prominent, vertical headlamps. Little wonder that the SL quickly became an icon of style and speed, the ultimate blend of glamour and performance, regarded as a classic in its own time. In 1999 the Gullwing 300SL was voted 'Sports Car of the Century' in an international poll and still these rare and dramatic cars continue to fetch high prices at auction – amply demonstrating that, almost half a century after its introduction, the Gullwing legend was as strong as ever.

4 SL Roadsters – The Cars to Be Seen In

At the 1954 International Motor Sports Show in New York most eyes had been on the spectacular new Mercedes-Benz 300SL Gullwing road car, which was making its debut. But next to it on the Mercedes stand was the prototype of a car that in some ways was just as significant – and would certainly be seen on the roads rather more frequently. Relying on existing production components even more heavily than the 300SL had done, and looking very much like its elder brother, this was a relatively cheap open-topped sports car with which Mercedes-Benz hoped to cash in on the 300SL's image. It was also the first road-going Mercedes roadster of the post-war era, introducing a new facet to the SL brand. The new car was the 190SL.

While the 300SL had been designed as a racing car and had then been refined into a road-going production machine with encouragement from American distributor Max Hoffman, the new 190SL was first and foremost a road car, which had been designed to be cheap and easy to build. It was based on the 180 saloon that had been introduced the previous year, the saloon bringing with it two new concepts for Mercedes road cars. The first was the full-width or 'pontoon' body, lacking the old-fashioned separate wings of earlier cars. The new body gave the cars their common nickname of *Ponton*, German for pontoon. The second new feature was the concept of 'unitary' construction, where the chassis members are built into the floor and

form an integral part of the body instead of being a separate structure with an unstressed body on top. A good unitary structure liberates more passenger space from a given size of car and, because in a unitary structure the body itself shares some of the load, the whole car can be made stiffer, stronger and, at the same time, lighter in weight. Lighter weight was certainly a priority for the 180, because it was still powered by the old pushrod engine from the 170Sb, developing just 52bhp.

For the new sports car more than 10in (250mm) was chopped out of the saloon's wheelbase and the whole structure stiffened to compensate for the loss of a fixed roof. Thanks to the strong floor structure, conventional doors with low sills could be used to make ingress and egress somewhat easier than with the 300SL. Luggage space was considerably better too, with a usable boot at the back rather than a glorified spare wheel orifice.

At the front of the car a subframe carried the engine, gearbox, suspension and steering just as it did on the 180 saloon, making both production and major overhauls simpler and quicker. The subframe also improved refinement, because its three-point rubber mounting helped to damp out road shocks and vibration. The front suspension itself was by the same proven system of twin unequal-length wishbones, coil springs and telescopic dampers that had been used on the 170 and 180 saloons, with the addition of an anti-roll bar. At the back, the prototype 190SL was

The Ponton *180 saloon donated its platform and suspension to the 190SL, but not its engine.*

The 190SL *was deliberately styled to look like the Gullwing 300SL, so that some of the faster car's image might rub off on the cheaper roadster.*

initially given the 180's swing-axle suspension layout, with a single-point chassis mounting for the final-drive unit and rubber-bushed trailing arms picking up on the drum brake back-plates on either side to handle some of the driving and braking forces. This meant the axle shafts themselves did not have to be so robust and the result was a useful saving in unsprung weight. It was a system that had been tested on the 300SL racer, though in the end it had not been adopted when the road-going Gullwing went into production.

The 180 had been given much smaller diameter wheels than the outgoing 170, with 6.40 × 13 cross-ply tyres which had been specially developed to wear just as well as the previous 16in covers. The 190SL followed suit and the 13in wheels considerably improved the car's handling, thanks to a further reduction in unsprung weight. The smaller wheels

and tyres also contributed to a lower centre of gravity and a lower rear suspension roll-centre. In the braking department the 190SL departed from its saloon forebear with broader brake shoes and 'turbo-cooled' brake drums – similar to those on the 300SL, but in cast iron rather than aluminium.

Clearly the 190SL needed more power than the 180's paltry 52bhp, so under the bonnet was a new engine, designated M121. It was essentially a four-cylinder version of the over-head-cam six-cylinder M186, the 300 saloon engine that had provided the basis for the 300SL's power unit. That meant the light-alloy cylinder head was flat, with the combustion chambers being formed in the top of the iron block, and the single chain-driven cam operated two valves per cylinder using finger followers. An oil/water heat exchanger was fitted to help keep the oil cool. Unlike the 300SL

Swing Axles

Swing-axle rear suspension does a lot of good things and a few bad things, and as a result of the latter has received a great deal of bad press down the years.

With an old-fashioned live axle, the driven wheels are connected together via axle shafts and a differential unit, and the whole assembly is mounted on springs. Unsprung weight – everything attached to the suspension rather than to the body – is high, because it includes the heavy final drive unit. Traction can be poor, because the torque being applied to the final drive tries to turn the whole axle about the prop-shaft axis and that tries to lift one of the wheels off the ground. Because the axle connects the wheel on one side with that on the other, bumps affect both wheels rather than just one, so the ride is poor, and bumps under the inner wheel tend to push the more heavily loaded outer wheel into positive camber, thus reducing its grip on the road. And if all that wasn't enough the suspension designer's hands are tied because the roll-centre of the system cannot be changed.

The swing-axle layout is a simple way to make a big improvement. Here, the final drive unit is bolted to the chassis of the car and the driveshafts are given

joints at their inner ends, so the wheels can move up and down independently of each other and the final drive unit. The independently suspended wheels react better to bumps, and the chassis-mounted final drive reduces unsprung weight and deals with any torque reaction, improving traction.

But there is a big problem. If the driver panics mid-bend and closes the throttle or, worse still, hits the brakes, weight suddenly transfers to the front of the car and the back end rises on its springs. As the rear wheels droop on their driveshafts they assume a high level of positive camber, reducing the outside tyre's grip on the road. In extremis the back of the car tries to climb over the outside rear tyre, a phenomenon known as 'tucking under'. The result is a sudden loss of rear grip – and the car spins.

Limiting suspension travel and designing-in some static negative camber can help, while the Mercedes 'low pivot' design (where the axle casings are given a common pivot point below the differential) gave the half-axles a longer effective length and lowered the roll centre – both of which helped to reduce the 'jacking' effect.

installation, where the engine was canted over to the left, the 190SL engine was mounted vertically – there was just about room under that bulged bonnet, because the 190SL was a couple of inches taller than the 300SL. This time there was no expensive fuel injection system in the engine room: instead M121 was fuelled by a pair of twin-choke sidedraught Solex carburettors.

On a compression ratio of 8.5:1 – the poor quality of fuels available in the 1950s meant it could not be any higher without running into problems with pinking – M121 produced 105bhp at 5,700rpm, though the optimistic SAE 'gross' output was sometimes quoted at as much as 125bhp. Later a detuned version of the same engine (with a lower compression ratio, less aggressive valve timing and single-choke carburettors) provided a welcome power boost for the *Ponton* saloon.

Production Reality

Though the 190SL prototype had been seen alongside the new 300SL at New York early in 1954, the final production version of the road-ster would not appear until well over a year later. It was a busy time for the Daimler-Benz engineering teams, who were putting the final touches to the 300SL Gullwing road car, while at the same time developing the W196 for the new 2.5-litre Formula 1 and then the related 300SLR sports-racing car. On top of that had come the development of the important mass-market *Ponton* 180-series and 220-series models in a variety of guises with saloon, coupé and cabriolet bodies, and four-cylinder petrol, six-cylinder petrol and four-cylinder diesel engines.

By the time pilot production of the 190SL began in January 1955 the rear suspension had been updated. Mercedes' favourite swing-axle layout was retained, but now it was an improved low-pivot system first seen on the W196 racing car and then productionized for

the 220 saloon introduced in March 1954, the month after the New York show. In the low-pivot version of the swing axle the axle casings were extended under the final drive, where they were pinned together at a pivot point on the car's centre line – effectively extending the length of the half-axles and, as a result, reducing their ill-effects. One driveshaft was provided with a universal joint, as before, while the other was given a sliding, splined joint to take up the small axial movement that was a result of the common pivot point. Above the final drive unit sat a transverse coil spring, known as a 'balancing' or 'compensating' spring, which limited the camber angles that the wheels could adopt in an effort to keep them more or less vertical to the road surface. The new suspension made the 190SL more predictable near its limits than the 300SL had ever been and went a long way towards making up for the 190SL's lack of power compared to its six-cylinder stablemate.

Other changes from that initial show car to the final production machine included some restyling, to mirror the changes which turned the bitty-looking *Hobel* 300SL prototype into the much neater production-ready Gullwing, most noticeably a much more attractive front end. The radiator grille had been reshaped with rounded corners rather than *Hobel*'s sharp-cornered opening and the bonnet now stopped short of the front of the car, where the original had extended all the way to the grille. The bonnet also lost its original open scoop in favour of a neater, single bulge, which gave the front end a similar but not identical appearance to the Gullwing – and the bulge was, in any case, necessary to clear the overhead-cam engine's cambox. The 300SL-style wheel arch strakes, already adopted at the front of the 190SL, were now added at the rear too and the 'Mercedes-Benz' badges mounted on the prototype's front wings were removed for a cleaner appearance.

Though the production 190SL kept the

The low-pivot swing-axle used on the 190SL was first seen in production in the 220, which was available in saloon, coupé and convertible forms.

The 190SL's front-end styling was revised to give it much of the appearance of the 300SL. Note the single bonnet-bulge.

Without the raw performance of the 300SL or competitors from the likes of Porsche, the 190SL appealed to people who wanted the looks and quality without the drawbacks.

180's all-synchromesh four-speed gearbox, the decidedly unsporting column change of the saloon was dropped in favour of a short, remote gearchange lever between the front seats. Even so, for a sports car there were still some oddly pedestrian-looking features inside, such as the soft, wide seats, the big ivory-coloured steering wheel with its traditional chrome horn ring and spoke-mounted indicator controls, and the umbrella-handle handbrake under the dashboard. Trim and equipment were lavish for a 1950s sports car. A sophisticated heating and ventilation system provided individual controls for driver and passenger, there was proper carpeting, and a well-fitting convertible top made it as snug as any convertible car could be. The 190SL even had wind-up side windows, a refinement lacking in the much more expensive 300SL as a result of its curved, lightweight doors.

The 190SL-proper made its debut at the Geneva show in March 1955. At New York the previous year Mercedes-Benz had promised a price of less than $4,000 in the important American market and this they achieved – just. The 190SL went on sale in the USA at

The ivory-coloured steering wheel was typical Mercedes-Benz, as was the umbrella-handle handbrake under the dash.

1955–63 190SL

Chassis and body	Steel platform chassis with steel body
Engine	Front engine, longitudinal
Designation	1955–61: M121 B II
	1961–63: M121 B IX
Block material	Cast iron
Head material	Aluminium alloy
Cylinders	4 in-line
Cooling	Water
Lubrication	Wet sump
Bore × stroke	85 × 83.6mm
Capacity	1897cc
Main bearings	3
Valves/operation	Single chain-driven overhead camshaft, eight valves operated by finger followers
Compression ratio	1955–59: 8.5:1
	1959–63: 8.8:1
Fuel system	Two Solex 44PHH sidedraught carburettors
Maximum power	105bhp at 5,700rpm
Maximum torque	105lb ft at 3,200rpm
Transmission	Four-speed manual gearbox with synchromesh on all forward ratios. Rear-wheel drive
Gear ratios (1-2-3-4-R)	3.40-2.00-1.29-1.00-3.29
Clutch	Dry single-plate
Final drive ratio	3.70, 3.89 or 3.90
Suspension and steering	
Front	Double wishbones, coil springs, telescopic dampers, anti-roll bar
Rear	Single-pivot swing axle, coil springs, telescopic dampers
Steering	Recirculating ball
Wheels	5K × 13 steel disc wheels
Tyres	6.40 × 13 cross-ply
Brakes	Hydraulically operated drum brakes all round, with finned cast-iron drums
Dimensions	
Length	169in (4,293mm)
Width	68.5in (1,740mm)
Height	52.0in (1,321mm)
Track – front	56.3in (1,430mm)
Track – rear	58in (1,473mm)
Wheelbase	94.5in (2,400mm)
Unladen weight	2,508lb (1,140kg)
Performance	
Top speed	up to 112mph (180km/h) depending on axle ratio
Acceleration	0–60mph (97km/h) approximately 14.5sec

Though too heavy to be a competitive racing car, the 190SL was available with a kit to lighten and prepare it for racing.

$3,998, giving buyers the option of a Mercedes sports car with a purchase price considerably less than the 300SL Gullwing, for which Max Hoffman asked nearly $7,000. But though the 190SL was much cheaper than the Gullwing it still looked expensive compared to American and European rivals: Ford's Thunderbird 'personal car' started at well under $3,000, while the glassfibre-bodied Chevrolet Corvette and the fast and beautiful Jaguar XK120 could both be had for under $3,500. All of them were faster than the 190SL in a straight line, though none could offer the sophisticated all-independent suspension of the Mercedes.

The 190SL roadster with its convertible hood was joined by a coupé with a removable hardtop, which could be ordered with or without a hood to use in changeable weather. Also available was a kit to turn the 190SL into a more effective racing machine, this being an era when many road-going sports cars still led

double lives as weekday transport and weekend club racing cars. Fashionably cut-down doors were available and the full-width windscreen could be easily removed and replaced with a plexiglass aero-screen to reduce the frontal area. Lighter bucket seats were another option and the hood, bumpers and trim could also be removed to cut weight still further, but even in this form the 190SL was no racing car: it was far too heavy for that.

Even as a road car the 190SL cried out for more power, thanks to the more sure-footed handling provided by the new rear suspension. With 105bhp it was decently lively rather than genuinely sporting: several much cheaper British sports cars could leave the 190SL standing in a straight line, even if few of them boasted such sophisticated suspension to keep them in touch round the corners. Another rival, and a more expensive one than most of the British contingent, was the much racier

Porsche 356 built at Zuffenhausen, to the north of Stuttgart and just a few kilometres from Sindelfingen. Around the time the 190SL went into production, the 356 had been made available with a larger 1582cc engine with up to 75bhp and a more expensive 356 Carrera had been introduced using the four-cam engine from Porsche's successful 550RS racing car. The Carrera developed 100bhp from 1498cc – almost as much power as the 190SL, from little more than three quarters of the displacement – and weighing just 1,860lb (930kg) it was much swifter. By the time 190SL production ended in 1963, Porsche was selling a 2.0-litre Carrera with no less than 130bhp, way out of reach of the 190SL.

While the 1.9-litre engine of the 190SL had a respectable enough power output in this company – together with the flexibility, reliability and easy servicing that some competitors lacked – its all-up weight of more than 2,500lb (1,136kg) made its performance much more pedestrian than that of quicker competitors such as the Porsches. Instead the 190SL appealed to people who wanted Mercedes-Benz quality in an easy-to-drive open car that still combined comfort and convenience with a hint of sporting appeal, a tourer with some of the panache of the Gullwing 300SL rather than an out-and-out roadster. For those who wanted something quicker, a much more

powerful – and far more expensive – Mercedes roadster would soon appear.

Roadster revisions

Turning the 300SL Gullwing into an open roadster was the obvious next step. As Max Hoffman was quick to point out to Daimler-Benz, a folding roof would make the 300SL still more attractive in the convertible-crazy American market – and the company's management might also have been thinking that it would give them a competitor for Munich-based rival BMW's 507. Introduced at Frankfurt in 1955, the V8-powered BMW did not have quite the straight-line performance of the 300SL, nor its technical sophistication: though the engine that powered it was the first mass-produced all-alloy V8, it was fed by twin carburettors rather than fuel injection and had prosaic pushrod valve gear. The rear suspension eschewed Mercedes-style independence in favour of a simpler, torsion-sprung live axle. But the BMW was undeniably effective and made up for its comparatively simple engineering with a wonderfully curvy body, styled by Count Albrecht von Goertz (who had been encouraged to approach BMW by none other than Max Hoffman), and a removable hard top, which allowed open-air motoring with speed and style.

The 300SL Roadster that Mercedes-Benz

The 190SL provided much of the appeal of its bigger-engined cousins, lacking the shattering performance but lacking the phenomenal price tag, too.

BMW's V8-engined 507 must have been in Mercedes' minds during the development of the 300SL Roadster.

introduced in 1957 was much more than just a 300SL Gullwing with the roof removed, because the engineers also took the opportunity to make some improvements to the 300SL's design to answer criticisms of the original car. Many of the revisions centred on making the Roadster a more manageable and convenient road car than the Gullwing had been, as a result of its genesis as a racing car.

One of the areas of criticism of the 300SL coupé, ironically, was the gullwing-door arrangement that had captured the public's imagination so completely and which still marks out the coupé as something special today. Eye-catching though it undoubtedly was – there are few better ways to make an entrance than to arrive in a Gullwing and then raise those doors aloft to get out – in practice it meant that the 300SL coupé was not the easiest car to get into or out of, thanks to the high and wide sills dictated by the layout of the chassis tubes underneath. Ladies in narrow 1950s pencil skirts found demure entry and exit of a 300SL something of a challenge.

Drivers with deep enough pockets to afford an SL in the first place tended to be older and less athletic than the racing drivers the Gullwing SL had been designed for – and in any case, the drivers were paid to put up with it. Another worry was that the Gullwing doors provided little hope of escape if the car should overturn in an accident.

The 300SL racers had occasionally been run in 'roadster' form, with tiny doors that opened upwards and forwards, but conventional doors were an essential for a road-going convertible. The solution was to revise the chassis space-frame again, lowering the tubes at the sides of the chassis to reduce the height of the sills still further and allow deeper doors that could be hinged conventionally. Even then, the sills could not be perfectly flat, instead rising diagonally at the back of the opening to accommodate an essential chassis tube. The Roadster's doors were given more extensive internal trim and proper (frameless) side windows that wound down out of sight, rather than the Gullwing's fiddly removable panels. Reshaping the petrol tank and relocating the spare wheel (to a space under the boot floor) liberated some luggage space, which had always been restricted on the coupé.

The basic shape of a roadster body is much less stiff than that of a hard-top saloon or coupé, so when a coupé's roof is removed to make an open car a lot of work has to go into stiffening the chassis to avoid the result being a vibratory, ill-handling disaster. In the 300SL's case, the spaceframe chassis only extended upwards as far as the waistline of the car, so little strength was lost by the removal of the roof. But lowering the side members had a much more significant effect on the strength and, in particular, the stiffness of the chassis. Extra bracing had to be introduced into the front bulkhead and above the transmission tunnel to restore the stiffness; this successfully eliminated the 'scuttle shake' so common in open cars, where the whole structure of the car vibrates in sympathy with the suspension on a bumpy road – spoiling the carefully designed suspension geometry and upsetting

the passengers. The drawback to the restored chassis stiffness was an inevitable increase in weight, the Roadster weighing around 220lb (100kg) more than the coupé, despite lacking the earlier car's metal roof and heavy glass rear window.

Much of the criticism of the coupé had been about its tricky on-the-limit handling, thanks to the twin-pivot (or 'high pivot') swing-axle suspension at the back. The large variations in rear-wheel camber, track and roll centre position that the system allowed made for unpredictable behaviour on bumpy roads, and the 300SL needed a skilled and committed approach from the driver. For the 300SL Roadster, Daimler-Benz adopted the revised rear suspension arrangement that had been developed on the W196 racing cars and had already been seen in the production 190SL and the 220 saloon, with trailing arms to carry the braking and driving forces, a single pivot for the half-axles under the differential and a compensating spring to reduce camber change.

Michelin X radial tyres were now fitted as

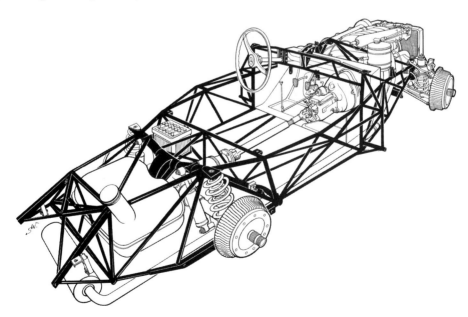

So that the 300SL Roadster could use conventional doors, the spaceframe chassis was revised to lower the sill height once again.

Apart from the open top, the Roadster also had a restyled front end and chrome strips highlighting the wing vents.

standard, improving the high-speed ride and offering more grip, though at the expense of some low-speed harshness and less progressive on-the-limit handling – undoing some of the good work done by the more effective rear suspension layout. But another change did improve the 300SL's user-friendliness: the steering, while still Mercedes' favourite recirculating ball, was now lower-geared. The race-derived Gullwing had needed little more than two turns of the steering from lock to lock, but the Roadster was given less sensitive steering, needing about three turns between

locks, to lighten the steering effort and make it a less nervous car to drive. Unfortunately the turning circle was still nearly 38ft (11.6m), on the unwieldy side when compared to the Volkswagen that most Germans drove (and which was only a few inches shorter than the Mercedes), which managed a much more compact 32ft (9.8m). The 190SL, actually 3in (75mm) longer than the 300SL Roadster but sitting on the same 94.5in (2,400mm) wheelbase, was a little more manoeuvrable with a 36ft (11m) turning circle.

The 300SL Roadster was clearly a much

Roadster on the Race Track

Paul O'Shea won the production sports car championship organized by the Sports Car Club of America (SCCA) in 1955 and 1956 using a Gullwing 300SL. For 1957, the plan had been to run a 300SL Roadster in the production car class to help promote the new road car, but the SCCA refused to admit the Roadster in the 'production' class, instead forcing it to run in Class D for more specialized sports-racing machines.

Up against purpose-built racing machinery the Roadster stood little chance in its production form. So Mercedes built a special '300SLS' Roadster for O'Shea, with looks reminiscent of the 1952 roadster-bodied W194s because the heavy bumpers were removed and the production wrap-around windscreen was replaced by a small aero-screen. A cockpit

cover was provided to smooth out the area above the redundant passenger seat and a roll hoop was provided behind the driver. The car had an aluminium-alloy cylinder block, fuel tank and steering column, a magnesium-alloy bell-housing, and drilled suspension components, all to cut weight. Thanks to the weight-saving programme the SLS tipped the scales at 2,293lb (1,040kg) fully fuelled, around 740lb (336kg) less than the production car.

Though not as fast as the Ferraris and Maseratis in the same championship, the 300SL proved to be very reliable, allowing O'Shea to win Class D of the championship with three times as many points as the runner up, Texan driver Carroll Shelby in a Maserati. It was the last major sporting victory for the 300SL.

easier car to live with than the Gullwing and a much easier car to drive fast than the earlier 300SL, which had demanded respect and skill from its driver if it was to cover the ground at speed and in safety. The Roadster generated little more outright grip on a smooth-surfaced race track, but it was much more predictable to drive on a bumpy real-world road.

Power at a Price

To help offset the increased weight of the revised car, the final drive ratio was shortened slightly, from 3.64:1 to 3.89:1, and the 'competition' camshaft that had been an option on the 300SL Gullwing was standard fit on the Roadster. Along with a higher compression ratio, up from 8.6:1 to a high 9.5:1 thanks to the continuing improvement in pump fuel, this helped the M198 engine develop a claimed 250bhp at 6,200rpm, with peak torque of 228lb ft at 5,000rpm – up from the Gullwing's 215bhp and 203lb ft. Even so, the Roadster was not quite as quick off the mark as the Gullwing. Nor could it match the more aerodynamic coupé's top speed, running out of steam at about 130mph (210km/h) compared to the Gullwing's maximum of 150mph (240km/h) or so when fitted with the standard 3.64:1 axle ratio. The difference in maximum speeds vindicated the original 1951 choice of a more aerodynamically efficient closed coupé for racing rather than the more common open sports car, but what mattered more to most road car customers was style.

The Roadster was still clearly related to the 300SL, but with some new additions and revisions to freshen up its appearance. The changes started right at the front of the car, where the headlight, fog light and turn indicator on each side were now combined into a single unit called a *Lichtenheit*. This was covered by a single glass lens on Roadsters destined for Britain and Continental Europe, while North American-spec cars had the same

lighting group but with a heavy chrome surround instead of the outer lens (which was outlawed in some states). The tall lighting unit tidied up the front end of the Roadster to give it a more sophisticated face and those vertical lights became something of a Mercedes trademark, reappearing on the *Heckflosse* (Fintail) saloons later in the decade and then on countless other Mercedes models during the 1960s and 1970s. At the back, the 300SL's rear light clusters were enlarged to incorporate reversing lights and US-market cars were given small additional reflectors.

Other visual changes included new horizontal chrome trims, which started at the wing vents and extended to the middle of the door on each side, and a windscreen with greater curvature. The change to the windscreen came for two reasons: the curve helped to keep the cockpit bluster-free when the car was driven with the soft top stowed and the side windows lowered, but also curvaceous windscreens with 'dog leg' A-pillars were trendy in

The Lichtenheit *light clusters made a big difference to the front end of the 300SL. Similar lamps would adorn uprange Mercedes models for the next fifteen years.*

73

1957–63 300SL Roadster W196 II

Chassis and body	Tubular steel spaceframe chassis with steel body
Engine	Front engine, longitudinal, tilted left at 45 degrees to vertical
Designation	1957–62: M198 I
	1962–63: M198 III
Block material	1957–62: Cast iron
	1962–63: Light-alloy
Head material	Aluminium alloy
Cylinders	6 in-line
Cooling	Water
Lubrication	Dry sump
Bore × stroke	85 × 88mm
Capacity	2996cc
Main bearings	7
Valves/operation	Single chain-driven overhead camshaft, twelve valves operated by finger followers
Compression ratio	8.55:1
Fuel system	Three Solex downdraught or twin-choke Weber sidedraught carburettors
Maximum power	215bhp at 5,800rpm
Maximum torque	203lb ft at 4,600rpm
Transmission	Four-speed manual gearbox with synchromesh on all forward ratios. Rear-wheel drive
Gear ratios (1-2-3-4-R)	3.34-1.97-1.39-1.00-2.73
Clutch	Dry single-plate
Final drive ratio	3.64 (3.25, 3.42 and 3.89 optional)
Suspension and steering	
Front	Double wishbones, coil springs, telescopic dampers, anti-roll bar
Rear	Single-pivot swing axle with compensating spring, coil springs, telescopic dampers
Steering	Recirculating ball
Wheels	Centre-lock steel disc wheels
Tyres	6.70 × 15 cross-ply
Brakes	1957–61: Hydraulically operated drum brakes all round, with finned light-alloy drums and vacuum servo
	1961–63: Hydraulically operated disc brakes all round with vacuum servo
Dimensions	
Length	179.9in (4,570mm)
Width	70.5in (1,790mm)
Height	51.2in (1,300mm)
Track – front	55.0in (1,397mm)
Track – rear	57.0in (1,448mm)
Wheelbase	94.5in (2,400mm)
Unladen weight	2,926lb (1,330kg)
Fuel tank capacity	22gal (100ltr)
Performance	
Top speed	up to 155mph (250km/h) depending on axle ratio
Acceleration	0–60mph (97km/h) approximately 10sec

the USA at the time and Mercedes were keen to win over the American market. The Fintail saloons that would replace the *Ponton* models in 1959 would also clearly reflect American tastes with their finned rear wings, though it turned out that their styling was not well received in the USA and sales of the saloon suffered accordingly.

Inside the Roadster, leather trim was now standard and leather also swathed the upper and lower surfaces of the dashboard, which was tidied up and fitted with revised instrumentation. The scatter of minor dials along the lower part of the Gullwing's dash – a slightly modified version of the W194's layout, which had also been repeated in the 190SL – was replaced by a tall rectangular combination instrument between the tachometer and speedometer, containing gauges for oil temperature, water temperature, oil pressure and fuel contents, plus a column of warning lights. Because the revised chassis now allowed lower sills, there was enough space for the driver to get in and out without there being need for either the removable steering wheel of the W194 racer or the tilting wheel of the Gullwing coupé.

Covering the 'office' was a very effective convertible roof, fully lined for better heat and noise insulation and impeccably made, as buyers naturally expected of Mercedes-Benz. When folded it dropped down out of sight into a well behind the seats, where the coupé's meagre luggage space had been, and was neatly covered by a hinged metal panel. Raising and lowering the roof was remarkably easy, so there was little excuse for missing out on sunny periods in Europe – or being caught in a rare shower in the sun-drenched states of the USA.

But all this extra style and convenience came at a significant premium: by the time the 300SL Roadster had reached the USA its price had broken through the $10,000 barrier – making it still more a car for the seriously rich.

Like the coupé, the Roadster had clean, aerodynamic lines. It looked good even with the roof up.

The wrap-around windscreen helped protect passengers from the wind with the roof down.

Like the Gullwing before it, the Roadster became one of the cars that rich and famous people wanted to be seen in: a car for Hollywood stars, playboys and millionaires. It was glamorous enough to steal the show as

Inside, the 300SL was much as before, except that the minor instruments were grouped into a block in-between the main dials. There was a now a glovebox for the passenger and wind-down windows.

Improvements to the rear suspension made the 300SL Roadster much more stable and easier to handle than the coupé, particularly on bumpy roads.

Though not quite as quick in a straight line as its predecessor, the Roadster was more comfortable and more usable – which is what mattered to most customers.

The Celebrities' Favourite

Both the 300SL Gullwing and Roadster attracted customers with household names. King Hussein of Jordan had a 300SL, as did film stars Tony Curtis and Sophia Loren. Canadian jazz pianist Oscar Peterson bought one of the last Roadsters in 1962 and kept it until the 1980s. Comedian Tony Hancock became a Roadster customer in May 1960, though his car suffered a more dramatic fate: while Hancock was being driven home by his wife after recording an episode of his TV series *Hancock* in June 1961, the Mercedes crashed in some ill-lit roadworks, leaving the pair of them badly shaken and Hancock with a pair of black eyes. As a result he was unable to learn his lines for the next episode, called *The Blood Donor*, and read most of them off cue cards.

Motor racing personalities were also 300SL customers. The great Juan Manuel Fangio was presented with a metallic-blue Roadster by Daimler-Benz at the London Motor Show at Earls Court in 1959. Fangio used the hard-top car in Europe until 1960 and then had it shipped to his native Argentina, where he continued to run it for some years. Apparently local traffic never did get used to its performance. In Europe one of the first customers for the 300SL Gullwing had been Scotch whisky magnate and racing team proprietor Rob Walker, who was driving his Mercedes (with its distinctive 'ROB 2' registration number) in January 1959 when he came upon Mike Hawthorn in his 3.8 Jaguar. Being the racers they were, they were soon travelling quite quickly – too fast for Hawthorn, as it turned out, because shortly after overtaking Walker's Mercedes he lost control of the Jaguar. It hit a tree and the new Formula 1 World Champion was killed instantly.

effectively as any Ferrari and, on a more practical level, it was rather more reliable and easier to live with than most Italian machines.

Few major changes were made over the car's seven-year production life. A removable hard top was introduced as an option in 1958 to make the car a more attractive 'every-day' in the winter; in hard-top form it was known as the 300SL Coupé. In 1961 Daimler-Benz finally overcame its reservations about the new-fangled disc brakes that were by now standard fit on Jaguars, Ferraris, Aston Martins and other high-performance cars, and the 300SL's old-fashioned drums were replaced by Dunlop discs at all four corners. Then, in March 1962, the M198 engine was given an alloy cylinder-block to reduce weight.

Like its more powerful stablemate, the 190SL changed only in detail during its production run – slightly modified carburation, a

When production of the 300SL Roadster ended in 1963, it marked the end of the spaceframe SLs, first seen in 1952.

lower third gear, a minor increase in compression ratio and the bigger tail-lights of the 220 saloons. The rear number-plate lamps were moved into the over-riders in 1957 and the previously optional over-riders made standard – though front over-riders remained an extra-cost option. The only other noticeable change was an enlarged rear window for hard-top models, partly to improve rear three-quarter vision and partly to make the 190SL's hardtop look more like that available for the 300SL Roadster, to strengthen the visual connection between the two cars. By 1963, when production of both SL roadsters ended, the 190SL had sold 25,881 cars and carved out a niche for Mercedes-Benz as a maker of quality convert-

ibles for the well-heeled (one of the last 190SLs would have set you back around $6,000 in the USA) in addition to the shatteringly fast and expensive performance cars it made for enthusiasts.

The 300SL Roadster had shown that Mercedes-Benz was making even such rapid cars easier and more convenient to use, an idea that struck a chord with 1,858 buyers between the car's introduction in 1957 and the end of production in 1963. It was a theme that would be explored still further in the next generation of SLs, which Uhlenhaut and his team had been developing since 1958. Those new SLs were now just around the corner.

Today the Roadster is not as sought-after as the iconic coupé, but is in many ways the better car.

One reinterpretation of the 300SL Roadster: Mercedes-Benz asked film and music personalities to design their own colour schemes and this is what Britney Spears came up with.

5   Pagoda –
The Sophisticated Sports Car

Both the Gullwing and Roadster forms of the 300SL betrayed their race-car origins all too clearly. They were ferociously fast in a straight line, but relatively noisy and uncomfortable, capable of high cornering speeds but tricky to drive at the limit – unless you had the car control skills of a Moss or a Fangio. They were also phenomenally expensive and not terribly practical: boot space was minimal, and they were difficult cars to get into and out of, although the Roadster had been much better than the Gullwing in both areas. If you needed something more practical, but wanted to remain a Mercedes customer, then the only alternative was the 190SL, which was much more affordable but much slower.

Other cars were catching up. More and more Ferraris were now built and trimmed to road-going standards, with more comfortable interiors and bigger, torquier engines. Jaguar's XK120 had evolved into the XK140 and XK150, setting new standards of luxury and refinement in 'Grand Touring' cars. Its strikingly-styled and very fast D-type racing car pointed the way to the road-going Jaguars of the future. Another British racing marque, Aston Martin, had moved up a gear by replacing its DB MkIII with the rapid and beautiful DB4, complete with a brand new all-alloy, twin-overhead-cam straight-six engine. The latest V8-engined Corvettes – while not in the same league as Mercedes in quality, image or handling terms – were now starting to compete in straight-line speed. Meanwhile,

American V8s were being used in European expresses like the Facel Vega, giving them an appealing blend of effortless power and traditional coachbuilt quality.

So when work began in October 1958 on the car that would eventually replace the 300SL Roadster, it was clear that the outcome would be a very different machine. The new SL had to be more user-friendly – a practical car with space and good visibility, easy to drive and with forgiving handling. Unlike the tricky 300SL, it had to be able to make good progress in trying conditions without requiring the driver to be both talented and well-trained. It also had to be a more comfortable car: anyone with enough money to buy a 300SL was used to being pampered by luxury cars, and was not prepared to sacrifice a good ride and a welcoming interior even in a sporting car.

Converging Styles

The replacement for the 300SL would be no remodelled racing car. For one thing, Mercedes-Benz had given up racing at the end of 1955, in the aftermath of the terrible accident at Le Mans involving Pierre Levegh's 300SLR. For another, sports racing cars were now so far removed from road cars that it was almost impossible to make a practical road-going machine and an effective racing car from the same basic design, as Uhlenhaut and his team had done with the 300SL in 1953. Starting with a clean sheet of paper meant that there was no need for the new SL to be compromised by racing car origins: it could be a purpose-built road car from the word go.

What the new car needed was to blend the speed and panache of the 300SL with some of the best qualities of the 190SL – its neater handling, its convenience and, hopefully, its ease of manufacture. If all that could be blended into one package, not only would the new car be a step forward from the old 300SL, it would also be an effective replacement for the 190SL. The concept was quickly approved: a single new SL, known by its Daimler-Benz design code of W113, would be introduced to replace both the old cars at a stroke.

After four years of development the new SL made its debut at the Geneva Salon in March 1963, the same show that had seen the debut of Jaguar's E-type two years earlier. While the Jaguar was clearly a product of its maker's racing activities in the 1950s, the Mercedes was a completely new departure with a very different appearance to the outgoing 300SL Road-

ster. The tall *Lichteinheit* lamp units (also now in use on the faster Fintails and the big 600) were retained and the new SL was given a new version of the wide, low air-intake that had become an SL trademark, again carrying a big Mercedes-Benz star and a horizontal chrome band. But there the resemblance to the old SL ended. Where the old SL's lines had been a confluence of curves that celebrated speed, the new car was crisply angular like a fashionable Italian suit. The line of the front wings was carried back almost horizontally for the length of the car, broken only by a hint of a shoulder behind the door. Gone were the side vents, the twin bonnet bulges and the 'eyebrows' over the wheel arches. Instead the new SL was clean and conservative, well-proportioned and elegant – though its drag coefficient of 0.51 was nothing to shout about after the paragon of streamlining that had been the 300SL.

The soft top contributed to the elegance of the car, by folding away out of site under a neat metal cover. The new hardtop was naturally

'The elegant sports car with its new-look styling,' said Mercedes-Benz. The 230SL's clean-cut shape was a radical departure from the curves of the 300SL it replaced.

Béla Barényi's safety ideas reached production in the Heckflosse or 'Fintail' saloons in 1959.

given the same clean and angular style as the rest of the car, but controversially it also incorporated a dip in the centre of the roof panel, which was very obvious when viewed from dead ahead or astern. It was an idea that had come from engineer Béla Barényi, who suggested that a curve would add stiffness to the roof panel. There was also talk that the raised edges of the roof also meant that the glass area could be greater for better visibility and allow easier entry to the car without incurring the drawback of a much greater frontal area – but the real reason for the shape was that it contributed to the SL's effortlessly elegant styling. Some observers thought it reminded them of roofs on Chinese buildings and, as a result, the car quickly earned itself the nickname of 'Pagoda roof'.

Under the Skin

Barényi had been involved in much more than just the design of the roof. Safety was now an important consideration at Sindelfingen and an enormous amount of crash test analysis had been carried out during the 1950s, intended to make its cars safer for their occupants in accidents. Barényi's revolutionary 'crumple zone' safety concept had gone into production in the new 220 Fintail saloon, which had replaced the six-cylinder models at the top of the *Ponton* series in 1959. Just as the 190SL's underpinnings had been derived from the 180 saloon nearly a decade earlier, now the Fintail would provide the running gear and the safety concept for the new SL.

W113 carried over much of the Fintail's chassis and body engineering. Like the 190SL

Almost all cars are now based around the concept of the rigid safety cell with crush zones front and rear, pioneered by the 'Fintail' Mercedes saloon and then adopted on the W113 SL.

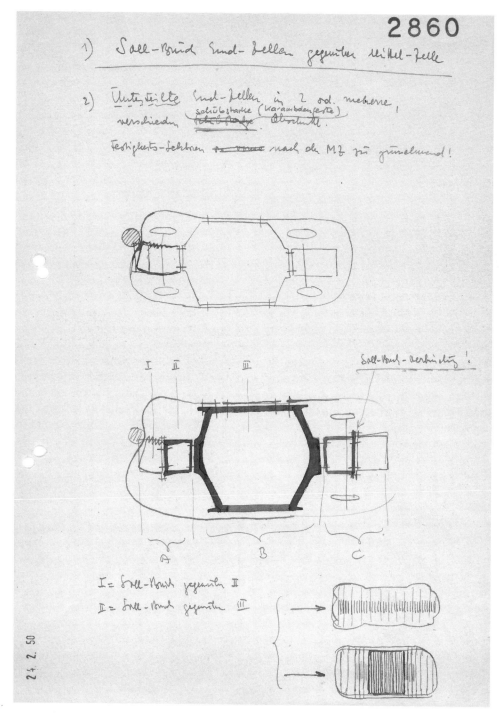

As these original notes show, the 'safety cell' concept used crush zones front and rear to protect a rigid passenger compartment.

Analysis of real accidents provided much of the data for early Mercedes-Benz safety work.

there was no separate chassis, the body being welded to a strong floorpan that incorporated stress-bearing members. The floorpan was based on that of the saloon, but was around 14in (350mm) shorter, so that the new SL could retain the 94.5in (2,400mm) wheelbase of both the 300SL and 190SL. The chassis and body were designed to take advantage of the 'crumple zone' principle, making the W113 the first sports car in the world with this new safety technology.

The basic suspension design was also carried over from the saloon, and was essentially a development of the layout seen in the *Ponton* saloon and 190SL. The proven system of unequal length double-wishbones and coil springs (plus an anti-roll torsion bar) suspended

the front end, while at the back there was the single-pivot swing axle that had been used on the previous SLs and had then been incorporated into the Fintail saloon. Despite being so much shorter than the saloon the SL retained the Fintail's 58.5in (1,485mm) track. Though the new car was about 9in (229mm) shorter than the old 300SL, its tracks were 4in (100mm) and 2in (50mm) wider at the front and rear respectively, giving it the potential for better handling than the old SLs.

Uhlenhaut's quest for a better-behaved SL began with the tyres. Though radial tyres were now available, the technology was still in its infancy and radials had serious drawbacks – the worst of them being the lack of feedback they gave as they approached the limit of

Béla Barényi and the 'Crumple Zone'

Safety engineering was already an important part of the work going on at Daimler-Benz in the late 1940s and one of its guiding lights was engineer Béla Barényi. In 1948 Barényi presented a concept he called 'Terracruiser', for a car of the future, and with it came the beginnings of an idea that would revolutionize safety design in cars.

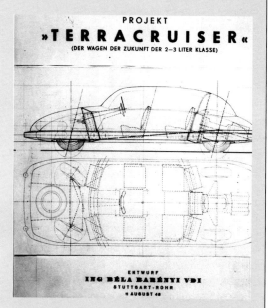

Barényi's Terracruiser concept for a family car of the future incorporated innovative safety ideas.

Béla Barényi, the engineer whose safety ideas revolutionized car design. The 'Pagoda-roof' SL was one of the first cars to benefit from his 'safety cell' concept.

Until the 1950s it had been thought that the best way to offer protection to a car's occupants during a collision was to make the car as strong as possible. Barényi realized that a much more effective way of avoiding injury was to allow the car to deform in a controlled way to dissipate the kinetic energy, reducing the decelerations suffered by the occupants. The concept he drew up included a strong central 'safety cell' containing the occupants, protected at either end by what became known as 'crumple zones'.

Daimler-Benz applied for a patent for Barényi's concept in 1951 and eight years later applied it in production in the Fintail saloons. In 1963, the 230SL became the first sports car with the new safety technology, which has since become the standard method of designing-in crash protection in conventionally-sized cars. As an aside, the tiny Mercedes-engineered Smart turns the idea on its head by having no crumple zones, instead incorporating a very strong outer frame that is intended to activate the crumple zone of any vehicle it hits.

Barényi did not stop there, later working on several other important safety innovations including the collapsible steering column, the impact-absorbing steering wheel, pedestrian-friendly hidden windscreen wipers and side impact protection. By the end of his career he had more than 2,500 patents to his name.

adhesion. Uhlenhaut wanted a blend of high performance and user friendliness, which meant blending the characteristics of both cross-ply and radial tyre.

Daimler-Benz approached two tyre companies, Firestone and Continental, to create bespoke tyres for the W113. Uhlenhaut wanted tyres with the grip of a radial, but the breakaway characteristics of a cross-ply, good steering response and a comfortable ride. The section width was to be 185mm (7.2in) – which seems narrow today, but was then daringly wide – and the tyres would include special scuff-protection ribs to prevent damage to the sidewalls. The result was what Continental called the *Halbgürtel* or 'half belt' tyre, very nearly but not quite a proper radial, because the reinforcing plies were not absolutely radial but, instead, at a slight angle. This stiffened the sidewalls, giving better steering response and better feedback, while still keeping its rayon-braced tread flat on the road for exceptional cornering grip. The wide track also helped and at the back the longer swing axles were less susceptible to the curious

camber changes that had bedevilled the 300SL coupé. The SL was more predictable than ever, while at the same time delivering a comfortable and well-damped ride.

Smooth and Sufficient Power

Just as the chassis and suspension had been derived from the new 220 saloon, so was the engine. The 2195cc M127 engine in the 220 had been carried over from the *Ponton* series, with revised valve gear and new valve timing. It was an overhead-cam in-line six with a wide 80mm bore and short 72.8mm stroke and all-alloy construction, using a four-bearing crankshaft that helped to avoid the torsional vibration problems that in-line sixes were prone to, but still allowed the engine to rev freely. M127 was designed to be an efficient and powerful unit of relatively small capacity, capable of providing a heavy saloon car with decent performance without incurring high levels of tax that were imposed on bigger engines in some markets. Through a combination of punctilious engineering and high-

Tyre Technicalities

During the life of the 300SL there had been significant strides forward in tyre technology and one of the main advances had been the development of the radial tyre.

Until the 1940s, the standard 'cross ply' car tyre incorporated layers or 'plies' of fabric that reinforced the tyre carcase, the cords of the fabric on each side being laid at 45 degrees to the tread centreline to form a trellis pattern. In 1946, Michelin patented a new design of 'radial ply' tyre, where the cords of the reinforcing material were disposed radially, travelling from one tyre bead, through the sidewall, under the tread and through the opposite sidewall to the other tyre bead. The Michelin design also incorporated inextensible steel bracing for the tread.

The radial tyre proved to have significant advantages. Because the stiff tread was mounted on flexible sidewalls, the tyre kept its tread flat to the road during

high-speed cornering. By contrast the tread and sidewalls in a cross-ply tyre were of similar stiffness, so in cornering the whole tyre would deform and at least part of the tread would leave the road. As a result the radial offered much higher levels of grip. High-speed ride was also particularly good and radial tyres ran cool, making them suitable for the sustained high-speed running that was becoming possible with high-performance cars and newly emerging motorway networks. But there were drawbacks: at low speeds the radial was harsher than the cross-ply because of its reinforced tread and when the radial finally reached its limit it tended to break away with little warning.

For the new SL, Rudolf Uhlenhaut wanted a tyre with the grip and stability of a radial, but with the gentle breakaway characteristics of a cross-ply. The tyres that resulted were something of a compromise between the two technologies.

Like the 300SL, the 230SL's six-cylinder engine was fuel injected – though this time the injectors were in the ports rather than the cylinder walls.

quality manufacture it was capable of a high specific output and, at the same time, displayed the imperturbable reliability that had become a Mercedes trademark.

In the six-cylinder 220 Fintails, later known as the 220b to avoid confusion with the earlier *Ponton* 220, the M127 engine was available in three different states of tune and quickly won a reputation for smoothness and flexibility. It developed 95bhp in its most basic twin-carb form in the 220b, rising to 110bhp in the 220Sb and 120bhp in the fuel-injected 220SEb. For the SL, the engine was bored out by 2mm to 82mm while the stroke was left unchanged, to give a capacity of 2306cc. The compression ratio also rose from 8.7:1 to 9.3:1.

It was installed vertically in the SL, giving the new car one more thing in common with the 190SL, rather than the 300SL.

This new version of the engine used fuel injection, of course, but in a different form to that seen on either the previous 300SL or the 220SE. Mercedes-Benz had now moved away from the diesel-like 300SL system, where fuel was injected directly into the cylinder using a six-plunger pump driven at half engine-speed. Instead the 220 had injectors placed in the intake manifold, operated by a much cheaper two-plunger pump running at engine speed and delivering fuel through a pair of metering blocks, each of which controlled three cylinders. For the new 230SL another different system was employed: now there was a six-plunger injection pump running at half engine-speed and the injectors were placed in the cylinder head, squirting fuel into the intake ports.

All this gave the 230SL considerably more power than the 220SE, with a peak output of 150bhp at 5,500rpm, together with excellent smoothness throughout the rev-range – which was just as well, because the engine gave of its best when it was revved hard. What it did not do was match the output of the old 300SL, the new 2.3-litre engine being some 70bhp down on the old 3.0 litre – though it was a good 45bhp more than the 190SL, amply demonstrating how the new one-model SL range was a compromise between the two older cars.

But is it a Sports Car?

That lack of power in comparison to its more illustrious predecessors led some commentators to doubt the sporting nature of the latest Mercedes roadster and other elements of the car's specification added weight to their theories. As an alternative to the conventional four-speed manual gearbox (which was provided with a handily-placed remote gearchange lever between the seats) customers could order a four-speed, fully-automatic transmission. Since 1956 Mercedes-Benz had made American Borg-Warner automatic transmissions available on the 300c and 300d saloons, and had also offered Hydrak automatic clutches as options on the *Ponton* and Fintail cars. In 1961 the Hydrak option was replaced by a Mercedes-built four-speed automatic and this transmission was now made available on the 230SL, in which form the car could also be specified with hydraulic power steering. Die-hard sports car fanatics scoffed at power assistance but, as so often, they missed the point: the assistance meant the steering ratio could be more direct, making the 230SL more wieldy to handle.

As if the technical specification wasn't enough to make sports car purists fume, the interior appointments of the 230SL made it clear that this was no stripped-out road-legal racing car. Instead the quality of trim and level of equipment inside the SL reflected the wishes of the clientele Mercedes-Benz aimed to attract. The dashboard was adorned with fashionable chrome and trimmed in leather, and leather could also be ordered as an alternative to the standard vinyl facings for the seats. There was the usual huge Mercedes steering wheel complete with chrome horn ring and padded 'safety' boss, and an ovalized rim to give the driver's legs more space. In contrast to the array of instruments seen in most sports cars, the 230SL came with a development of the instrument layout seen in the 190SL and the Fintail saloon, with the circular speedometer and tachometer split by a combination instrument containing rectangular gauges for oil pressure, temperatures and fuel contents. Minor controls like the indicators and windscreen wipers were now grouped on a new multi-function steering-column stalk.

Everything about the 230SL seemed to make life far too easy for it to be a proper sports car. The doors were wide for ease of entry and exit, the accommodation spacious and comfortable, there was provision for oddments and effective weather protection whether the hard top or soft top was in use. A rear seat designed to accommodate a single, transverse passenger could even be specified, to make the car still more versatile. But thoroughly civilized as it may have been, the 230SL was still a sports car – and Mercedes-Benz sought to prove it with a press launch at the tiny racing circuit of Montroux in France, near the Swiss border.

Naturally, Rudolf Uhlenhaut was on hand to prove that the new 230SL had all the grip and handling prowess that should be expected of a sports car. Also there on the day was Mike Parkes, who combined careers as a racing

Restrained luxury was the theme inside the 230SL. Trim quality was high, the seats were comfortable and ventilation top-class.

driver and development engineer for Ferrari in the way one suspects Uhlenhaut would have liked to do for Mercedes-Benz. Parkes regularly raced Ferrari's 250GTO in GT events, occasionally appeared in their Formula 1 machinery and, a couple of years earlier, he had finished second at Le Mans in a Ferrari Testa Rossa that he had shared with Willy Mairesse. That day at Montroux, Parkes was testing a 240bhp 250GT Berlinetta, recording a best lap time of 47.3 seconds for the twisty 0.7 mile track. Once Uhlenhaut was in his stride, he got the 230SL down to 47.5sec.

Further proof that this was a properly sporting Mercedes came shortly after the launch, when Mercedes works driver Eugen Böhringer and navigator Klaus Kaiser entered a 230SL in the demanding Spa–Sofia–Liège – the 'Marathon de la Route' that, until 1962, had been the Liège–Rome–Liége and had been won twice by 300SLs. Böhringer had identified the new SL as the ideal mount, smaller and more wieldy than the big 220SE that he had used the previous year. Competitions manager Karl Kling agreed and an SL was built up with the standard four-speed manual transmission, power steering, and a lower 4.56:1 final drive. Careful engine preparation yielded 167bhp and an oil cooler was added for reliability. Three driving lights were fitted at the front, while inside Halda Twinmaster and Speedpilot instruments were added, bucket seats fitted and the pedals rearranged to suit Böhringer better, but the

huge standard steering wheel was retained. More specialized equipment included a Very signalling pistol – just in case the SL crashed down a ravine, though there were rumours that it also came in handy when trying to overtake trucks trailing huge clouds of dust on some of the unmade East European roads.

Supremely elegant, the Pagoda-roof SL quickly became a style icon.

Béla Barényi with the 230SL on show in 1963.

Supremely elegant in any setting, the 230SL was also swift across country, thanks to its tidy handling.

Böhringer and Kaiser won the Spa–Sofia–Liège rally shortly after the 230SL was announced – settling any arguments about whether or not the new SL was a 'sports car'.

Eugen Böhringer

Today Eugen Böhringer is still famous for his achievements behind the wheels of Mercedes-Benz touring cars in rallying and circuit racing. Yet Böhringer did not take up motor sport until the age of 36 and his career at the top level lasted barely five years.

Eugen Böhringer put Mercedes on the rallying map, and gave the 230SL a winning start.

He was born in Stuttgart on 22 January 1922. The family ran a restaurant just outside the town, though young Eugen's father had previously worked at 'the

Daimler'. Consequently Böhringer trained as a chef until the outbreak of war, spending three years in military service and a further seven in captivity during which he sustained severe leg injuries in a mining accident. He returned to Stuttgart in the late 1940s, later taking over the family business.

Motor sport didn't enter the picture until 1958, when Böhringer entered the Solitude Rally after a bet with some of his regular customers. To everyone's surprise he finished second.

By 1960, Böhringer had earned a works seat at Mercedes-Benz, driving the Fintail saloons in rallies, hillclimbs and circuit races. Böhringer proved to be adept at all these disciplines and particularly effective in endurance events, where his fitness and stamina paid dividends.

Böhringer recorded three wins in the Polish Rally, two in the Spa–Sofia–Liège (the second one, in 1963, at the wheel of the new 230SL) and twice in the Gran Premio de l'Argentina. Other rally victories included the Acropolis (twice) and the German Rally, plus five class wins on the Monte Carlo Rally. He was European Rally Champion in 1962.

In circuit racing he won touring car titles at the Nürburgring and Macau in 1964, and numerous other races, including 24-hour endurance events at Spa-Francorchamps.

Böhringer entered fewer events after 1963, but now at the age of 81 he still remains closely linked to Mercedes-Benz, recently driving a replica of his 1963 230SL and often seen at the wheel of his own 300SL Roadster.

Böhringer opted for 15in wheels to give the SL greater ground clearance on the rough roads of the Yugoslavian stages, which he said had 'stones the size of footballs'. The SL was then switched to 13in wheels for the smoother roads through the Alps, to lower the gearing and improve acceleration. The biggest challenge to the Mercedes came from an Austin-Healey 3000 entered by the BMC works rally team, but once that crashed out of the event Böhringer and Kaiser were left to win comfortably, despite running out of brakes on the

way down the notorious Stelvio pass. It was just the fillip the new SL needed, proving at a stroke that the 'Pagoda-roof' SL was both civilized and competitive.

Bigger and Better

Little changed on the W113 until May 1966, when a ZF five-speed gearbox was made available as an option at a premium of DM1,200. That was just the start of a flurry of activity on the SL front because, less than a year later, the

From this angle the 'Pagoda' roof looks more conventional. The contrasting colour scheme was popular in the 1960s.

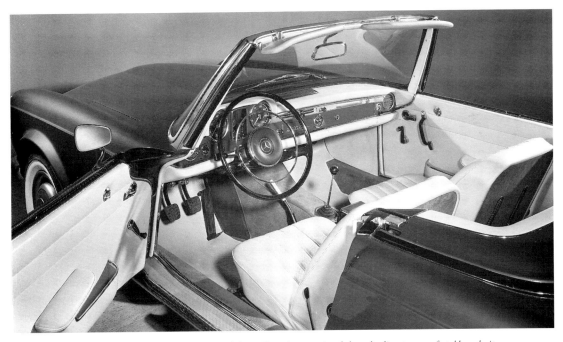

The 'Pagoda-roof' SL was much easier to get into, with low sills and conventional doors leading to a comfortable cockpit.

With the roof stowed under a metal cover, the W113 SL displayed a clean unbroken line from stem to stern.

The 250's bigger engine had more torque, but the car looked identical to the 230. Note that this W113 has no soft top and that two suitcases fill the space behind the front seats.

230SL was replaced by the 250SL, which inherited a larger seven-bearing, straight-six engine from the W108 250SE saloon that had appeared in 1965. M129, as it was known, derived its extra 190cc capacity from a 6mm-longer stroke, boosting the engine's torque peak by about 10 per cent but leaving maximum power at 150bhp. Changes elsewhere on the car included a larger fuel tank for longer range between refills, and modifications to the braking system, with larger front pads, discs rather than drums at the rear and a pressure-proportioning valve to avoid rear-

wheel lock-up. The major change to the way the car drove was not an increase in performance, but rather a reduction in the effort required from the driver: the bigger engine was much more flexible, and Mercedes-Benz offered a longer rear-axle ratio as an option to take advantage of the improved torque.

Thus far the SL had been available in three forms – as a roadster (fitted with just a soft top), as a hard-top only coupé, and as a coupé with both a removable hard top *and* a soft top underneath. For the Geneva show in March 1967, Mercedes-Benz introduced a fourth

Only the 250SL's boot badge gave away the extra capacity of the engine. Within a year the model was replaced by the 280SL.

variant, with a hard-top roof and a pair of rear seats taking up the space liberated by leaving out the soft top.

Bigger news came early the following year, when the 250SL was replaced by the 280SL. Starting with the 2.5-litre M129 engine, Mercedes moved the bore centres slightly further apart to accommodate 86.5mm bores. With the stroke still at 78.8mm the capacity was now 2778cc and the power output had risen to 170bhp. But it wasn't all good news, because the stronger engine now started to show up the limitations of the chassis – and the chassis was no longer what it had been. Rubber bushes had been incorporated into the suspension to avoid the 230SL's need for regreasing every 2,000 miles (3,200km), with the side-effect that some of the old sharpness had been lost. More conventional tyres were now used, too, and the result was that the 280SL seemed to lack the precision of its forebears.

The 280SL also introduced numerous minor safety improvements. Interior lighting was improved, three-point seat belts were fitted and the release handles for the hard and

From the front, the concave roof is very evident. The 280SL was less demanding of suspension maintenance, but the rubber bushes in it compromised its handling.

Professor Béla Barényi with a 280SL in 1996. The fancy wheel trims are the only obvious difference between the 280 and the earlier models.

soft tops were made detachable so they did not need to remain attached to the header rail where they could cause injury in an accident. It all served to demonstrate very clearly some of the challenges for the sports car in the 1970s: safety would be a top priority.

The 'Pagoda-roof' SL certainly had its critics. Those who judged it merely by looking at it were apt to dismiss it as nothing more than a boulevard cruiser, undoubtedly elegant but lacking in substance. Those who drove it told a different story, reporting that the SL of the 1960s was every bit as serious a motor car as its predecessors had been. By the time its eight years of production came to an end in March 1971, the 'Pagoda-roof' SL had

sold 48,912 units, which proved that Mercedes had accurately assessed its market.

But that market was changing. While the 230SL had undoubtedly been one of the most civilized sports cars ever made, the character of its successors had become softer and softer. The biggest selling of the three 'Pagoda-roof' SLs had been the 280, and 77 per cent of the Pagoda SLs had been supplied with automatic transmission. Buyers wanted Mercedes sports cars to deliver performance, certainly, but with ever greater convenience and comfort. The car that would replace the W113 would do exactly that, and as a result it would sell in far greater numbers – and for far longer.

94

Like the earlier W113s, the 280SL was often fitted with automatic transmission – a sign of things to come.

Inside, as out, the 280SL was much the same as its predecessors. This is an automatic car – note the serpentine gear-shift quadrant on the floor.

Available with a soft top and a removable hard-top, the 'Pagoda-roof' SL was a versatile machine.

The V8 Pagoda

The big 300 'Adenauer' saloons of the 1950s were replaced in 1963 by the even bigger Mercedes-Benz 600, which quickly picked up the *Grosser Mercedes* soubriquet of a pre-war counterpart. It was powered by a new 6.3-litre V8 engine – the first V8 in Mercedes' history – and in the mid-1960s Erich Waxenberger, the manager of the experimental department, had one of the big V8s inserted into an S-class saloon. When Rudolf Uhlenhaut heard the V8 S-class go past his office window late one evening he demanded to drive it and when he returned from the drive, suitably impressed, the pair pressed Daimler-Benz management to put the car into production. The result was the 300SEL 6.3, introduced at the Geneva show in March 1968.

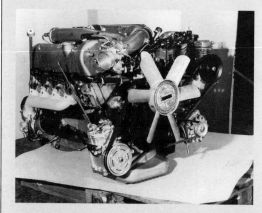

One 'Pagoda-roof' SL was fitted with this – the 6.3-litre V8 engine from the enormous 600 limousine. The chassis was barely able to cope.

While this car was under development, Waxenberger and Uhlenhaut decided to create a Pagoda-*über-alles* by shoehorning the huge V8 engine into the front. Extensive changes were required to make room for the engine, amongst them a re-routed steering linkage, but the only external clues to this SL's secret were two fat exhaust pipes and a vast bulge in the bonnet to clear the V8's injection equipment.

Compared to the 170bhp of the contemporary 280SL, the V8 delivered no less than 250bhp at 4,000rpm, with the colossal maximum torque of 369lb ft occurring at 2,800rpm. Despite the extra weight of the bigger engine this gave W113/12, as the car was known internally, a power-to-weight ratio of around 165bhp/tonne – not quite in the same class as the old 300SL, but a significant improvement on the 280's 126bhp/tonne. Uhlenhaut claimed the sprint to 100km/h (62mph) from rest took around seven seconds and, if anything, it was probably quicker than that. W113/12 could reach 140mph (225km/h) and, running on Dunlop racing tyres, it recorded a lap of the Nürburgring Nordschleife in 10min 30sec.

But it wasn't all good news. That big iron-block V8 made the Pagoda nose-heavy and weight-transfer to the front during hard braking overloaded the front tyres – while the prodigious torque all too easily overwhelmed grip at the rear. Anti-dive and anti-squat suspension geometry might have helped, but that wouldn't make its appearance until the R107 SLs of the 1970s.

Another W113 was fitted with a 203bhp Wankel rotary engine, giving the Pagoda a top speed of 127mph (205km/h) – but like the V8 Pagoda, the rotary-engined car never made it into production.

The 1952 racing 300SL was remarkably successful and went on to be the basis for the Gullwing road car.

The 300SL racer's cockpit was more civilized than most racers', with full trim and effective ventilation.

Rudolf Uhlenhaut's 'Competition Coupé' SLR was probably the fastest car on the roads in the 1950s.

With its gullwing doors the Competition Coupé looks a lot like a 300SL, but it has more in common with the 300SLR sports-racer.

The Production 300SL shared the racer's gullwing doors and spaceframe chassis – and added fuel injection, too.

This rear view of the 300SL shows off the aerodynamically clean lines to advantage.

The road car's cockpit was similar to the racer's, but sported an optional leather trim and (not visible here) a luggage space behind the seats.

300SL Roadster and Gullwing share the Mercedes-Benz museum with the 300 saloon and cabriolet models from which their engines and suspension were derived.

The 300SL Roadster – though its spaceframe chassis was superficially similar, there were extensive changes to allow lower sills without compromising stiffness.

The 'baby brother' of the 300SL, the 190SL shared its stablemate's smooth aerodynamic lines. That it has just one bulge in the bonnet rather than two shows that, under the skin, things weren't quite the same.

The new 'Pagoda roof' SL (this is a 230SL) replaced both the 190SL and 300SL models in 1963. It continued the 300SL Roadster's front-end styling, with a wide grille and tall light units.

'Pagoda roof' SL in the Mercedes-Benz Museum, in the company of an S-class (left) and 600 (right).

Eugen Böhringer secured a famous victory in the 1963 Spa–Sofia–Liège rally to put the 'Pagoda roof' SL firmly on the map. This is a replica of the original rally car.

The third-generation 350SL emphasized even more the width and low height of the SL family.

The 420SL appeared in 1985, featuring bigger wheels with low-profile tyres.

The SLC was a family of fixed hard-top coupés, which ran from 1972 to 1981

The 300SL-24 of the 1990s retained the clean, understated lines that had served Mercedes so well over the previous four decades.

Three special edition models were introduced right at the end of R129 production in 2001. From left: designo Alanite, Silver Arrow and designo Almandine.

The new R230 SL reXects Mercedes' house style while still having its own clear identity.

Glass panel option makes the folding 'Vario roof' even more versatile.

The latest SL body has much more surface interest than its rather slab-sided predecessor.

230SL/250SL/280SL W113

Chassis and body	Steel platform chassis with steel body
Engine	Front engine, longitudinal
Designation	230SL: M127 II
	250SL: M129 III
	280SL: M130
Block material	Cast iron
Head material	Aluminium alloy
Cylinders	6 in-line
Cooling	Water
Lubrication	Wet sump
Bore × stroke	230SL: 82 × 72.8mm
	250SL: 82 × 78.8mm
	280SL 86.5 × 78.8mm
Capacity	230SL: 2306cc
	250SL: 2496cc
	280SL: 2778cc
Main bearings	230SL: 4
	250SL/280SL: 7
Valves/operation	Single chain-driven overhead camshaft, twelve valves operated by finger followers
Compression ratio	230SL: 9.3:1
	250SL/280SL: 9.5:1
Fuel system	Manifold fuel injection, mechanically controlled, Bosch 6-plunger pump
Maximum power	230SL/250SL: 150bhp at 5,500rpm
	280SL: 170bhp at 5,750rpm
Maximum torque	230SL: 145lb ft at 4,200rpm
	250SL: 159lb ft at 4,200rpm
	280SL: 177lb ft at 4,500rpm
Transmission	Four-speed manual gearbox with synchromesh on all forward ratios. Optional four-speed automatic. Revised gearing and optional five-speed box from 1965. Rear-wheel drive
Type	Four-speed manual, 230SL 1963–65
Gear ratios (1-2-3-4-R)	4.42-2.28-1.53-1.00-3.92
Clutch	Dry single-plate
Final-drive ratio	3.75:1
Type	Four-speed manual, 230SL/250SL 1965–68
Gear ratios (1-2-3-4-R)	4.05-2.23-1.40-1.00-3.58
Clutch	Dry single-plate
Final-drive ratio	230SL: 3.75:1; 250SL/280SL: 3.92:1 (3.69:1 optional, standard from 1970)
Type	Five-speed manual, optional on 230SL/250SL 1965–68
Gear ratios (1-2-3-4-5-R)	3.92-2.22-1.42-1.00-0.85-3.49
Clutch	Dry single-plate
Final-drive ratio	4.08:1 (late 280SL: 3.92:1)
Type	Four-speed automatic, optional
Gear ratios (1-2-3-4-R)	3.98-2.52-1.58-1.00-4.15
Coupling	Fluid coupling
Final-drive ratio	230SL: 3.75:1
	250SL 3.92:1 (3.69 optional, standard from 1970)

230SL/250SL/280SL W113 *continued*

Suspension and steering

Front	Double wishbones, coil springs, telescopic dampers, anti-roll bar
Rear	Single-pivot swing axle, coil springs, telescopic dampers
Steering	Recirculating ball
Wheels	Steel disc wheels
	230SL: 5½J × 14
	250SL/280SL: 6J × 14
Tyres	185HR14 radial
Brakes	Hydraulically operated dual circuit system, with vacuum servo
	230SL: disc front, drum rear
	250SL: discs front and rear

Dimensions

Length	169in (4,292.6mm)
Width	69.3in (1,760mm)
Height	52.0in (1,321mm)
Track – front	230SL: 58.5in (1,486mm)
	250SL/280SL: 58.4in (1,483mm)
Track – rear	230SL: 58.5in (1,486mm)
	250SL/280SL: 58.5in (1,486mm)
Wheelbase	94.5in (2,400mm)
Unladen weight	2,849–2,992lb (1,295–1,360kg)
Fuel tank capacity	230SL: 14.3gal (65ltr)
	250SL/280SL: 18.0gal (82ltr)

Performance

Top speed	230SL: up to 124mph (200km/h) depending on axle ratio
	250SL: up to 124mph (200km/h) depending on axle ratio
	280SL: 124mph (200km/h)
Acceleration	230SL: 0–62mph (100km/h): 9.7sec
	250SL: 0–62mph (100km/h): 9.7sec
	280SL: 0–62mph (100km/h): 9.0sec

6 *Panzerwagen* – Refining the SL Idea

With a new decade came a new set of worries for sports car makers the world over. No longer was it enough to build sporting cars with scorching straight-line speed, powerful braking, glue-like grip and precise handling. All cars were now called upon to be more responsible, polluting the atmosphere less and looking after occupants and pedestrians better in collisions. Sports cars had to change and adapt, or die. With talk that American safety legislation might ban convertible cars altogether, there was much heated debate within Mercedes about the future of the SL: should the next model be a fixed-roof coupé as the original 300SL had been, or should the SL badge continue to be applied to a roadster, as it had been since 1957?

The 'Pagoda-roof' 280SL had already been witness to the first changes wrought by increasing public concern about pollution. For the USA the engine had been detuned with less aggressive valve timing and an over-run fuel cut-off system, both designed to reduce harmful emissions. But some states, notably California where the SL had been a big seller, now demanded yet more emission controls – threatening the high levels of performance that were part of the SL's appeal.

Though the new-generation SL was much the same size as its predecessor, it looked bigger and heavier.

The SL was offered with a soft-top roof, as here, and a removable hard-top. The ribbed tail lights stayed clean even in bad weather.

Safety had been a top priority in the design of the new SL. Here an R107 undergoes a rear impact test: note how the boot and rear wings have deformed, but the passenger compartment is still intact.

Safety was paramount, while refinement and comfort were ever higher on the list of priorities for Mercedes customers, as the popular 280SL had shown. These were all influences that made cars heavier and heavier, and with increased weight went duller acceleration, higher fuel consumption, more marginal braking and more ponderous handling. The only way to reconcile all these requirements was to start with a clean sheet of paper, which also provided the opportunity to deal with some of the criticisms that had begun to creep into reports about the old 280SL towards the end of its life.

Saloon Suspension

Some of those criticisms had centred around the 280SL's lack of handling precision compared to earlier models. Part of the problem was that the chassis now had to deal with a lot more tractive effort from the lustier 2.8-litre engine; there was also a limit to what the swing-axle rear suspension – even in its highly-developed, low-pivot form – could be expected to handle. But there was already a solution, which Mercedes had developed for the S-class saloons: there, the final drive was carried on a subframe that also provided wide-based pivot points for a pair of substantial semi-trailing arms. Springing and damping were handled by a combined coil spring/damper unit on each side (with a big bump stop that acted progressively as an 'auxiliary spring' near the limits of suspension travel) and an anti-roll bar. The semi-trailing arm design controlled camber changes much more effectively, reducing them by half compared to the old swing-axle design and, amongst other effects, the reduced camber change meant that the new SL could usefully employ the latest low-profile 70-series tyres. There were changes to the front suspension too, the usual unequal-length double wishbone suspension layout being retained, but with new geometry to give an 'anti-dive' effect, making the car more stable under braking. Not only did the car handle better than the old SL had done, it also provided an even smoother and better-controlled ride.

Also adopted from the S-class was a new engine and, for the first time, the SL moved away from in-line six-cylinder engines to embrace a V8. Clearly, greater capacity was needed as an answer to some of the quicker rivals, such as the 3.8-litre and 4.2-litre Jaguars, but a bigger-capacity straight-six would have been longer and less space-efficient. A longer engine also made it more difficult to fit in the all-important front crush-zone. So instead of a straight-six, Mercedes went for a V8.

The first Mercedes-Benz V8 had been a mammoth 6.3-litre unit for the 600 limousine, which had been introduced six months after the 'Pagoda-roof' SL in 1963. For the new S-class saloon, and ultimately the next generation of SL, a more compact 3.5-litre V8 was designed using some of the lessons learned from the earlier unit. The block was cast iron rather than aluminium alloy, after tests revealed that the 66lb (30kg) weight saving from an alloy block was negated by the weight of extra sound-proofing required due to the block's poor sound-deadening properties. With a cast-iron block the engine was quieter, stronger and potentially more reliable.

Like the previous six-cylinder engines, the V8 – known as M116 – was significantly over-square, with a bore of 92mm and a stroke of just 65.8mm. The short stroke kept the block compact, and also meant that high engine speeds could be attained without undue stress. Indeed, the whole engine was designed with strength and reliability in mind: generously-sized main and big-end bearings were specified, the crankcase extended well below the crankshaft centreline to ensure the whole engine was strong, and the crank and connecting rods were bullet-proof forged steel.

The 350SL's iron-block V8 engine came from the 280SE 3.5. Essentially the same engine, in different capacities, would power the R107 throughout its long production life.

The big bore meant there was plenty of space for large valves, so the engine could breathe well. The two big valves in each combustion chamber were operated by chain-driven overhead camshaft on each bank of cylinders via finger followers in the usual Mercedes style. Less conventional was the control of ignition and fuel injection, with transistorized ignition and the new Bosch Jetronic injection using solenoid-operated injectors. The more precise control of combustion that these systems offered helped M116 to meet its emissions targets and, at the same time, develop 200bhp, just 50bhp behind the much larger V8

in the 600. In the saloons the V8 had been partnered by a three-speed automatic transmission with a hydraulic torque-converter, which multiplied torque at low road speeds to help acceleration. The SL, by contrast, had the older four-speed automatic with a simpler fluid flywheel (lacking the rotating third element of the torque converter). At this stage there was no manual gearbox option.

So the new SL certainly had plenty of power from its 3.5-litre V8, but that was only in Europe. To get through the tough certification process that was essential before the car was allowed to go on sale in the USA, the V8 engine needed lower compression, weaker mixtures, new cam-profiles and revised ignition timing, along with careful control of crankcase ventilation. The only way to restore the power sapped by these emissions controls was to increase the capacity, which was done by taking the stroke out to 85mm to give a swept volume of 4520cc. That done, the 'desmogged' engine only just about produced as much power as the 'dirty' 3.5-litre engine for Europe, though it did offer a higher torque maximum at low revs and, as a result, had to be fitted with the three-speed automatic gearbox, the only one Mercedes had with a high enough torque capacity.

New Style

The new car was christened the 350SL, following the usual Mercedes practice where the type number denotes the engine size – though, confusingly, the 4.5-litre car for the USA was known as a 350SL 4.5, not a 450SL. The boardroom battles between the coupé and roadster camps had been resolved in favour of the latter, but the new car, project R107, was given an almost completely new appearance to its predecessor to ensure that even the most

technically uninterested customer realized that this was a very new motor car.

Though clearly a Mercedes, the 350SL carried over little of its predecessor's styling. At the front the headlamps were now horizontal rectangular units and outside them sat huge ribbed indicators, which were wrapped around the corners of the body so they were visible from in front and at the sides. The wide grille with its Mercedes star looked familiar, but above it was a new, bulbous bonnet stretching back to a swept-back windscreen with thick A-pillars, designed with the aid of computers to offer roll-over protection in an accident. The pillars were 50 per cent stronger than those of the previous car and the windscreen was bonded in to make the car even stronger, allowing the new SL to pass the 'roof drop' test without needing an additional roll-over bar. The pillars were also profiled to deflect rain water away from the side windows, keeping them clear in bad weather.

The 350SL sat on a wheelbase a couple of inches longer than the 'Pagoda-roof' 280SL, to provide more space in the cabin. Unlike the saloon-based platform of the Pagoda, the 350SL was designed from the ground up with a new floorpan, incorporating an enclosed

Light-alloy wheels, as fitted to this SL, were a costly option throughout the 1970s – but proved very popular.

propeller-shaft tunnel and box-shaped side members for additional rigidity. The longer wheelbase was accentuated visually by horizontal ribbing at the bottom of the wings and the doors to make the car look lower and sleeker, and more ribbing was applied to the tail lights – this time to help keep them clean. As on the previous SL, the soft top retracted into a hidden compartment to avoid sullying the car's lines when it was folded and the process of raising or stowing the roof took less than half a minute. The hard top carried over the 'Pagoda roof' profile of the previous SL and the boot lid was given a similar drooping profile to match.

There was a hint of a wedge shape to the new SL, a concession to a modern styling fashion but in only the subtlest of ways. Several more radical styling proposals were rejected in favour of a more conservative approach –

one that was to repay Mercedes many times over as the SL's production run stretched on and on.

Strong and Safe

New American regulations governing crash performance were making all cars that were to be sold in the USA heavier and the SL was no exception. Inside Mercedes it quickly acquired the nickname *Panzerwagen*, a reference to its tank-like strength – and weight. In its US specification the first of this new SL generation was more than 800lb (363kg) heavier than the first of the previous generation, thanks to a much stronger bodyshell and all-steel panels (some of the outer panels on the 'Pagoda-roof' SL had been aluminium alloy), with the doors designed to resist side impacts. In American spec the bumpers, too,

The wide grille and huge three-pointed star were by now an SL trademark.

One of the attractions of the SL was its versatile head gear. From left: removable hard-top, soft-top raised, soft-top lowered.

Like its predecessors, the R107 was a glamorous car that appealed to people who wanted to be seen.

R107 offered V8 engines, new rear suspension and much greater occupant safety than previous models.

were much larger and heavier because the car had to be able to withstand a 5mph (8km/h) front impact or 2.5mph (4km/h) rear impact without damage to any safety-related equipment, which included the fuel tank and lights. Even bigger bumpers would follow a couple of years later, as the regulations became ever more stringent.

There were safety innovations inside the SL too, and they applied in all markets. The dashboard now had three very clear and easy to read instruments grouped together in a binnacle ahead of the driver, and it was now covered with soft polyurethane mouldings to reduce the possibility of injury in a collision. The steering wheel retained the central crash-pad that Mercedes-Benz had developed in the 1960s, but now had four spokes and a moulded polyurethane rim to better protect the driver. Head restraints were fitted to the front seats as standard to help prevent whiplash injuries in the event of a rear-end collision. The 350SL even had a new type of seat belt – the 'inertia reel' – which automatically adjusted itself to the right length for any passenger and allowed the driver and passenger to move around in the cockpit, but locked automatically in a collision. Safer and far more convenient than the usual 'static' belts, they

drew widespread praise and were quickly adopted on other Mercedes-Benz models and by other manufacturers.

The larger interior that resulted from the slightly longer wheelbase meant there was space to plan-in an air-conditioning system, now vital for the American market, but the standard heating and ventilation system was typically thorough, too: even the insides of the door panels were warmed by the heater. More space was devoted to the 'occasional' rear seat, to make the accommodation a little more usable. Instead of the single transverse seat of the 'Pagoda-roof' SL, there was now space for two tiny rear seats, enough for small children. A padded bench was offered as an option, to make riding in the back a little more comfortable. Alternatively, the extra space provided a useful extra luggage area.

Like its predecessor, the R107 SL quickly became the kind of car in which the rich and famous were often seen. It was a convenient size, swift and surefooted, easy to drive and convenient to use. More importantly, perhaps, the three-pointed star on the front gave it the essential hallmark of quality and there was no doubting the style and good taste of the conservative design.

Leather trim was common, but the alternative tweed cloth was just as comfortable. For this picture the Mercedes photographer has removed the head restraints, which were standard on the R107.

Interior changes were relatively minor during the R107's long run.

SLC: Return of the Coupé

In June 1968, the Daimler-Benz board decided that the next generation of SL would be an open roadster, even though there had been disquiet in some quarters about possible American legislation banning open cars. Meanwhile Karl Wilfert, head of bodywork design at Sindelfingen, continued working on a fixed-roof coupé concept and succeeded in winning approval for the coupé to be produced alongside the SL roadster. It was announced at the Paris show in October 1971 as the 350SLC, replacing the saloon-based 280SE 3.5 coupé.

Crash testing continued during the cars' production run. Here an SLC reaches the end of the road against a concrete block.

The SLC's most elegant view was its profile, which showed the extra length of the wheelbase to good effect. The rear spoiler indicates that this car has one of the later alloy-block 5.0-litre V8s.

Up to the windscreen pillars it was all SL, both in styling and engineering terms, but in profile the SLC was quite different. It was 14in (360mm) longer, all of that going into an extended wheelbase that allowed room inside for better rear-seat accommodation. A slightly higher, convex roof-line (to improve head-room) blended into a huge, double-curved rear window, the boot lid being given a gentle convex profile to match. The long rear side-windows were fitted with controversial louvred panels leading into

the C-pillars: they were partly for style and partly to make the opening section of the window smaller, so there was enough space in front of the rear wheel-arch to allow it to drop down. In traditional Mercedes coupé style, there was no fixed B-pillar to interrupt the lines when all the side windows were wound down.

Though it was about 110lb (50kg) heavier than the SL, the SLC was near enough as fast in a straight line and, if anything, it had an advantage at high speeds thanks to a significantly improved drag coefficient. It handled better too, because of its longer wheelbase. Mostly it shared its engines with the SL, though when Mercedes-Benz went rallying in the late 1970s, the SLC was the first car to get the new alloy-block 5.0-litre V8.

In production for ten years, the SLC coupé sold 62,888 examples before being replaced by the SEC coupés derived from the new S-class saloon.

Coping with a Crisis

With the development of a larger-capacity engine to offset American emissions regulations, Mercedes had gone most of the way towards producing an even higher-performance SL for Europe. The 4.5-litre engine was presented in European specification at the Geneva show in March 1973 in the 450SL, developing

a lusty 225bhp. At the same time the US-spec 350SL 4.5 was renamed 450SL. In Europe the 350 and 450 ran parallel as a two-model range, the first time that SL customers had been given more than one choice of engine at a time.

But the 450SL arrived at just the wrong time. The Yom Kippur war strangled oil supplies to Europe, where petrol became scarce and

280SL/350SL/450SL

Chassis and body	Unitary steel body
Engine	Front engine, longitudinal. Three-way catalyst optional, standard from 1986
Designation	280SL: M110 E28
	350SL: M116 E35
	380SL: M116 E38
	450SL: M117 E45
	500SL: M117 E50
Block material	280SL/350SL/450SL: Cast iron
	380SL/500SL: Aluminium alloy
Head material	Aluminium alloy
Cylinders	280SL: 6 in-line
	350SL/380SL/450SL/500SL: V8
Cooling	Water
Lubrication	Wet sump
Bore × stroke	280SL: 86 × 78.8mm
	350SL: 92 × 65.8mm
	380SL: 1980–81 92 × 71.8mm, 1981–85 88 × 78.9mm
	450SL: 92 × 85mm
	500SL: 96.5 × 85mm
Capacity	280SL: 2746cc
	350SL: 3499cc
	380SL: 1980–81 3818cc, 1981–85 3839cc
	450SL: 4520cc
	500SL: 4973cc
Main bearings	280SL: 7
	350SL/380SL/450SL: 5
Valves/operation	280SL: Twin chain-driven overhead camshafts, twelve valves
	350SL/380SL/450SL/500SL: Single chain-driven overhead camshaft per cylinder bank, sixteen valves
Compression ratio	280SL: 9.0:1 (1976–78 8.7:1)
	350SL: 9.5:1 (1976–80 9.0:1)
	380SL: 1980–81 9.0:1, 1981–85 9.4:1
	450SL: 8.8:1
	500SL: 1980–81 8.8:1, 1981–85 9.2:1
Fuel system	Manifold fuel injection. 1974–76 Bosch D-Jetronic, 1976–85 Bosch K-Jetronic.
Maximum power	280SL: 185bhp @ 6,000rpm (1976–78 177bhp)
	350SL: 200bhp @ 5,800rpm
	380SL: 218bhp @ 5,500rpm (1981–85 204bhp @ 5,250rpm)
	450SL: 225bhp @ 5,000rpm
	500SL: 240bhp @ 5,000rpm (1981–85 231bhp @ 4,750rpm)
Maximum torque	280SL: 176lb ft @ 4,500rpm (1976–78 172lb ft)
	380SL: 220lb ft @ 4,000rpm (1981–85 232lb ft @ 3,250rpm)
	450SL: 279lb ft @ 3,000rpm (1975–80 266lb ft @ 3,250rpm)
	500SL: 297lb ft @ 3,200rpm (1981–85 298lb ft @ 3,000rpm)
Transmission	Rear-wheel drive
	280SL: Four-speed manual gearbox with synchromesh on all forward ratios, five-speed manual optional from 1976 and standard from 1981, four-speed automatic optional

280SL/350SL/450SL *continued*

	350SL: Four-speed manual gearbox standard, three-speed automatic optional
	380SL/500SL: Four-speed automatic gearbox standard
	450SL: Three-speed automatic standard
Type	Four-speed manual, 280SL 1974–77
Gear ratios (1-2-3-4-R)	3.90-2.30-1.41-1.00-3.66
Clutch	Dry single-plate
Final-drive ratio	3.69:1
Type	Four-speed manual, 280SL 1977–81
Gear ratios (1-2-3-4-R)	3.98-2.29-1.45-1.00-3.74
Clutch	Dry single-plate
Final-drive ratio	3.69:1 (3.58:1 from 1980)
Type	Four-speed manual, 350SL
Gear ratios (1-2-3-4-R)	3.96-2.34-1.44-1.00-3.72
Clutch	Dry single-plate
Final-drive ratio	3.46:1
Type	Five-speed manual, 280SL option 1974–76
Gear ratios (1-2-3-4-5-R)	3.96-2.34-1.44-1.00-0.875-3.72
Clutch	Dry single-plate
Final-drive ratio	3.92:1
Type	Five-speed manual, 280SL 1981–85
Gear ratios (1-2-3-4-5-R)	3.82-2.20-1.40-1.00-0.81-3.71
Clutch	Dry single-plate
Final-drive ratio	3.58:1
Type	Four-speed automatic, 280SL option 1974–80
Gear ratios (1-2-3-4-R)	3.98-2.39-1.46-1.00-5.47
Coupling	Torque converter
Final-drive ratio	3.69:1
Type	Four-speed automatic, 280SL option 1980–85, standard on 380SL/500SL
Gear ratios (1-2-3-4-R)	3.68-2.41-1.44-1.00-5.14
Coupling	Torque converter
Final-drive ratio	280SL: 3.58:1
	380SL: 1980–81 3.27:1, 1981–85 2.47:1
	500SL: 1980–81 2.72:1, 1981–85 2.24:1
Type	Three-speed automatic, 350SL option 1971–80, standard on 450SL
Gear ratios (1-2-3-R)	2.31-1.46-1.00-1.84
Coupling	Torque converter
Final-drive ratio	350SL: 3.46:1
	450SL: 3.07:1

Suspension and steering

Front	Double wishbones, coil springs, telescopic dampers, anti-roll bar
Rear	Semi-trailing arms, coil springs, telescopic dampers, anti-roll bar. Anti-squat geometry on 380SL/450SL
Steering	Recirculating ball, power assisted
Wheels	6½J × 14 steel wheels (light-alloy wheels optional)
Tyres	Radial
	280SL:185HR14 1974–80, 195/70HR14 1980–85
	350SL/380SL/450SL: 205/70VR14
Brakes	Hydraulically operated disc brakes all round with vacuum servo. Anti-lock system optional from 1980

280SL/350SL/450SL *continued*	
Dimensions	
Length	173in (4,390mm)
Width	70.5in (1,790mm)
Height	51.4in (1,300mm)
Track – front	57.7in (1,452mm)
Track – rear	57.7in (1,440mm)
Wheelbase	96.6in (2,460mm)
Unladen weight	3,307–3,483lb (1,500–1,580kg)
Fuel tank capacity	1974–81: 19.8gal (90ltr)
	1981–85: 18.7gal (85ltr)
Performance	
Top speed	280SL: 124mph (200km/h)
	350SL: 127mph (205km/h)
	450SL: 134mph (215km/h)
	500SL: 140mph (225km/h)
Acceleration	0–62mph (100km/h)
	280SL: 11sec
	350SL: 9.5sec
	450SL: 8.8sec
	500SL: 7.8sec

economies began to crumble. In Britain, a miners' strike led to a three-day week and petrol rationing coupons were issued, though they never had to be used in anger. Worse still, Value Added Tax was added to petrol in March 1974, by which time the price of a gallon of petrol had risen from 37p to 55p. Not only were large-engined thirsty cars expensive to run, they were seen as profligate and irresponsible.

The Mercedes response was to take the new 2.8-litre six-cylinder M110 engine from the S-class 280SE saloon and drop it into the SL. It was a fine engine, with a fully-counterbalanced seven-bearing crankshaft and torsional vibration damper, which made it exceptionally smooth, and a classic twin-overhead-cam top end with inclined valves and part-spherical combustion chambers, which made it very efficient. With an output of 185bhp it was only 15bhp behind the 3.5-litre V8, which was only fractionally more expensive to buy but much thirstier. The 280SL in full flight also generated the refined wail of a classic in-line six, which many preferred to the hard-edged burble of the V8, and some drivers were attracted by the availability of a manual gearbox for the first time in the R107 SL. Long after the fuel crisis had been forgotten, the 280SL still occupied a comfortable niche in the market and six-cylinder SLs would be available right through the model's production life.

Bigger V8s

While the V8s received updated injection systems, slightly reduced compression ratios (to meet stiffer European emissions regulations) and hydraulic valve-lifters (to cut maintenance requirements) over the next couple of years, the biggest news came in 1977 with the advent of a new V8 engine – and then it came in the SLC coupé rather than the SL. The long-term aim was to make the big S-class saloons lighter, swifter and, at the same time, more fuel efficient, which Mercedes planned to do by introducing aluminium cylinder-blocks. The low-volume SLC proved to be the ideal test bed for the new engine, because Mercedes could gain experience of the motor in service without exposing themselves to a major recall if there were problems – and at the same time the lighter aluminium-alloy block would help the rallying SLCs and the AMG racing cars to be a little more competitive.

The key to reducing weight had been to employ a new construction technique. Previously alloy-blocked engines had required cast-iron cylinder liners in order to provide dimensionally stable bores, but the liners were heavy, and their sealing and expansion rate compared to the block tended to present problems. The new block was chill-cast from a high-silicon alloy and the bores electrolytically etched to reveal large silicon crystals, which provided stable, low-friction bores. Because there were no liners, the engine was lighter by almost 90lb (41kg) and there was space for a wider bore: with a 96.5mm bore and 85mm stroke, the new engine displaced 4973cc and developed 240bhp at 5,000rpm, with 298lb ft of torque at 3,200rpm.

In the event, there was no need to worry about the reliability of the alloy V8, which quickly proved its worth in what was at first called the 450SLC 5.0, later the 500SLC. By 1980 the engine was also available in a 500SL, which, like the 500SLC, was given a deeper front air-dam and a small boot-lid spoiler to differentiate it from lesser models. At the same time the bonnet, boot lid and bumpers were swapped for aluminium items, in an effort to cut the cars' overall weight still further. A 380SL had now replaced the 350, using a smaller-capacity all-alloy V8 that had been introduced in the new W126 S-class saloons of 1979. Originally the 380 had retained the 92mm bore of the 350 and 450, but with a stroke that was between the two of them at 71.8mm. With a relatively short stroke and big

bore it had the free-revving character of the 350 and a power output of 218bhp, not far short of the old 450 and (perhaps more importantly) very similar to BMW's rival 3.5-litre six destined for its 6-series coupé.

For America the 380 had to be encumbered with the usual emissions gear, of course, but part of the programme of 'improvements' included slightly different dimensions, with a narrower 88mm bore and longer 78.9mm stroke. It arrived in America for the 1982 model year boasting just 155bhp, but that was only a whisker behind the outgoing US-spec 450SL, which had been progressively strangled by emissions laws until it could produce no more than 160bhp. Higher gearing, to improve fuel consumption, had also had a deleterious effect on performance. The 380 boasted the latest Mercedes four-speed transmission, which made it a fraction quicker in the benchmark 0–60mph (97km/h) sprint. The Americans had invented that performance measurement in the post-war years to demonstrate their cars' ability to regain cruising speed after stopping at a turnpike toll-booth. But the nation now had a blanket 55mph (89km/h) speed limit, so performance was something of an irrelevance.

At the same time the 'American' 380 dimensions were introduced into the European-spec car, trading a minor increase in maximum torque for a commensurate drop in peak power. The R107 SL had now been in production for eleven years and the SLC coupés had already been replaced by a pair of very American-looking four-seater coupés, the 380SEC and 500SEC, which were based on the new S-class saloons. Thoughts had turned to replacing the SL as early as 1979, but the roadster was still selling well. Despite styling that was conceived at the end of the 1960s and an unfashionably large dose of exterior chrome trim – matt black was now de rigueur elsewhere – the SL was as popular as ever. Quality and style were what mattered

Waxl's Competition SLCs

Though Mercedes-Benz retired from motor racing at the end of the tragic 1955 season, it retained some interest in rallying in the 1950s and 1960s, and that interest was reawakened in 1977. When the UK Mercedes-Benz importer decided to attempt the London to Sydney Marathon, Mercedes test department chief Erich Waxenberger offered to build the six cars, all 280Es. They were officially unofficial, but works cars in all but name with 'Waxl' and two of his best mechanics on hand to help. Two of the 280Es retired but the other four finished 1-2-6-8, with Andrew Cowan/Colin Malkin/Mike Broad winning the event outright.

The big SLCs were a handful on tight roads, but well-suited to long-distance marathons where their strength and reliability counted.

While Mercedes cars were too big for most of the European 'sprint' events, they clearly had potential on longer marathons. With the 5.0-litre SLC available for 1978, the team took on the South American Rally, a mammoth 18,000-mile (29,000km) thrash though all ten South American countries that lasted five weeks. The rules precluded major modifications to the engine, transmission or bodywork, but the team made such changes as they could under the tight regulations to give the SLCs a better chance of surviving. Duralumin shields were fitted under the engine and (automatic) transmission, to protect them on the rock-strewn roads, while the crew was protected by a tubular roll-cage and racing bucket-seats. The rear seat was removed to make space for tools, a fire extinguisher and a 120ltr (26.4gal) fuel tank. Oxygen was also carried, lest there be problems on the highest mountain passes, which climbed to more than 15,000ft (nearly 4,600m) above sea level. It was an

eventful rally: while the hugely experienced Timo Makinen managed to roll his SLC no less than three times, requiring major repairs at the roadside to keep him running, the reliable Cowan triumphed again.

Mercedes tuner AMG was now running highly modified SLCs on the track, but the works effort was still concentrated on rallying. Second place was the best the SLC could do on the Safari Rally in 1979, though it had been an organizational failure that had cost Hannu Mikkola a win, rather than any deficiency of car or driver. In December that year, SLCs took the first four places on the Ivory Coast Bandama Rally, with Mikkola at the head of the queue.

The alloy-block 5.0-litre engine made later SLC rally cars lighter and quicker.

The SLCs appeared in Portugal in March 1980 but were predictably outclassed by lighter, more manoeuvrable cars – though faultless reliability meant Bjorn Waldegaard and Ingvar Carlsson could finish fourth and fifth as other cars failed. But cracked trailing arms delayed the Mercedes in the Safari Rally and Mikkola's co-driver, Arne Hertz, was hit by another car while the SLC was being repaired, Vic Preston salvaging some honour with third place behind two Datsuns. There were retirements in the Acropolis Rally and more in Argentina, where the surviving Mikkola/Hertz SLC finished second. Mikkola again led the Mercedes challenge in New Zealand, finishing third, while the three SLCs of Carlsson, Cowan and Waldegaard were delayed by accidents. The SLCs went out on a high, Waldegaard winning the 1980 Bandama Rally – with Mercedes' retirement from rallying being announced just a few days later. After a few short seasons back in competition, the three-pointed star was once again absent from motor sport.

This press shot, intended to show the SL's spacious boot, also gives a good view of the ribbed, stay-clean tail lights.

and the SL had that aplenty, even if, for America at least, it no longer had the performance expected of a sports car.

It was common knowledge that Mercedes-Benz was now working on a successor to the R107 and most commentators felt that the 1982 revisions would be the last before the old SL was phased out. Yet, by 1985, there was still no sign of a brand new SL and Mercedes-Benz was announcing a whole raft of changes and improvements to the old one – including yet more new engines.

114

Capacities increased at the same time the alloy-block engines were introduced: the boot-lid badge indicates that this is the 380SL.

The 500SL was much the same as the previous 450SL, except for the engine – and the black spoiler on the boot-lid.

By the 1980s the SL's extensive use of exterior brightwork was starting to look dated.

Roof down the R107 was still a handsome car…

…and the effect was not diminished with the hard top in place.

Revisions in 1986 included a new air dam under the front bumper.

SL Swansong

Though it had only been on sale since 1980, the 380SL was replaced by a 420SL, which combined the 92mm bore of the earlier V8s with the 78.9mm stroke that had been used in the later 380s. Bigger valves and more efficient ports aided breathing and the engine was now fuelled by computer-controlled Bosch KE-Jetronic injection. With the three-way exhaust catalyst that would soon become standard fit, the 420SL delivered 204bhp at 5,200rpm and 224lb ft of torque at 3,600rpm. The 500 also received bigger valves and new cam-profiles to operate them, boosting its power output to 245bhp (or 223bhp in catalyst-equipped form). At the other end of the range the now-venerable twin-cam 2.8-litre six was replaced by a single-cam 3.0-litre engine, which had been introduced in the new W124 mid-size saloons at the end of 1984, reintroducing the '300SL' nomenclature after a gap of nearly a quarter of a century.

The SLs that appeared for 1986 were given more than just revised engines. Most notice-able to the casual observer was that the light-alloy wheels were now a sleeker design (to fit in with the modern trend towards more aero-dynamically efficient body shapes) and an inch larger in diameter. They carried lower-profile tyres, now 205/65VR15, and created enough space at the front for larger, ventilated brake discs and four-pot calipers. Anti-lock braking was now standard, bringing the highest profile (but oldest) Mercedes model into line with the rest of the range. The suspension geometry of the S-class saloons was adopted at the front, while anti-squat geometry at the back kept the V8s level while accelerating. That trend towards wind-cheating shapes also allowed Mercedes to add a deep front air-dam that reduced front-end lift by a third – just a few years earlier it would have looked very strange indeed. The interior, too, would have looked strange to the SL buyer of a few years earlier: there was now wider use of polished wood trim, the seats were fatter (though that meant there was less space in the cabin) and the hub of the four-spoke steering wheel was now fat with an air bag.

300SL/420SL/500SL/560SL	
Chassis and body	Unitary steel body
Engine	Front engine, longitudinal. Three-way catalyst optional, standard from 1986
Designation	300SL: M103 E30
	420SL: M116 E42
	500SL: M117 E50
	560SL: M117 E60
Block material	300SL: Cast iron
	420SL/500SL/560SL: aluminium alloy
Head material	Aluminium alloy
Cylinders	300SL: 6 in-line
	420SL/500SL/560SL: V8
Cooling	Water
Lubrication	Wet sump
Bore × stroke	300SL: 88.5 × 80.25mm
	420SL: 92.0 × 78.9mm
	500SL: 96.5 × 85.0mm
	560SL: 96.5 × 85mm
Capacity	300SL: 2962cc
	420SL: 4196cc
	500SL: 4973cc
	560SL: 5547cc
Main bearings	300SL: 7
	420SL/500SL/560SL: 5
Valves/operation	300SL: Single chain-driven overhead camshaft, twelve valves
	420SL/500SL/560SL: Single chain-driven overhead camshaft per cylinder bank, sixteen valves
Compression ratio	300SL: 9.2:1
	420SL/500SL/560SL: 9.0:1
Fuel system	Bosch KE-Jetronic manifold fuel injection, mechanical/electrical control
Maximum power*	300SL: 180bhp @ 5,700rpm
	420SL: 204bhp @ 5,200rpm
	500SL: 223bhp @ 4,700rpm
	560SL: 230bhp @ 4,750rpm
Maximum torque*	300SL: 184lb ft @ 4,400rpm
	420SL: 224lb ft @ 3,600rpm
	500SL: 264lb ft @ 3,500rpm
	560SL: 275lb ft @ 3,250rpm
Transmission	Rear-wheel drive
	300SL: Five-speed manual gearbox with synchromesh on all forward ratios. Four-speed automatic optional
	420SL/500SL/560SL: Four-speed automatic standard
Type	Five-speed manual, 300SL
Gear ratios (1-2-3-4-5-R)	3.86-2.18-1.38-1.00-0.80-4.22
Clutch	Dry single-plate
Final-drive ratio	3.46:1
Type	Four-speed automatic, 300SL/420SL
Gear ratios (1-2-3-4-R)	3.86-2.41-1.44-1.00-5.14
Coupling	Torque converter

300SL/420SL/500SL/560SL *continued*

Final-drive ratio	300SL: 3.46:1
	420SL/560SL: 2.47:1
	500SL: 2.24:1
Suspension and steering	
Front	Double wishbones, coil springs, telescopic dampers, anti-roll bar
Rear	Semi-trailing arms, coil springs, telescopic dampers, anti-roll bar. Anti-squat geometry on 420SL/500SL/560SL
Steering	Recirculating ball, power assisted
Wheels	7J × 15 light-alloy wheels
Tyres	205/65VR15 radial
Brakes	Hydraulically operated disc brakes all round with vacuum servo. Anti-lock system optional on 300SL, standard from 1986. Standard on 420SL, 500SL and 560SL
Dimensions	
Length	173in (4,394mm)
Width	70.5in (1,790mm)
Height	51.4in (1,306mm)
Track – front	57.7in (1,466mm)
Track – rear	57.7in (1,466mm)
Wheelbase	96.6in (2,454mm)
Unladen weight	3,329–3,781lb (1,510–1,715kg)
Fuel tank capacity	18.7gal (85ltr)
Performance	
Top speed	300SL: 126mph (203km/h)
	420SL: 132mph (213km/h)
	500SL: 141mph (225km/h)
	560SL: 139mph (223km/h)
Acceleration	0–62mph (100km/h)
	300SL: 9.6sec
	420SL: 8.5sec
	500SL: 7.3sec
	560SL: 7.7sec

*Note: figures shown are for catalyst-equipped models. Maximum power and torque for non-catalyst versions (where available) were typically 5–10 per cent higher.

Across in America there was to be just one more SL model, which would redress the balance in performance terms between the US- and European-spec SLs. 'Grey' imports to the USA of the much quicker European-spec SLs had grown during the 1980s, as wealthy customers wanted the best there was, rather than just what Mercedes-Benz was willing or able to supply. Because the V8 engine had already been expanded to 5.6 litres for the S-class by increasing the stroke to no less than 94.8mm, there was no problem producing a US-only 560SL with all the latest chassis refinements and an emissions-friendly 5.6-litre engine, which Mercedes launched onto the US market in 1986. Until then the fastest American-spec SL had been the very first 350SL 4.5 back in 1971, but the new 560 boasted 227bhp (at only 4,750rpm) and 279lb ft of torque – making it a much swifter sprinter (with a 0–60mph (97km/h) time of around 7.5sec, a couple of seconds quicker than the US-spec 350SL) even if it was no quicker at the top end. The respected American

The new air dam and 'aerodynamic' wheels gave the fifteen-year-old SL shape a new lease of life.

After a seventeen-year absence, the 300SL returned: this time it was powered by the single-cam straight-six engine from the W124 saloon.

120

The 500SL still topped the European SL range, offering a blend of performance and docility that was hard to match.

With the hard top in place the 500SL was a snug saloon, but the roof was as heavy as ever.

The new air dam blended surprisingly well with the SL's basic shape, which was now in its teens. Reduced lift at speed and lower fuel-consumption were the major benefits.

The 'SRS' legend on the steering wheel indicates the presence of an air bag. By the end of the eighties, the R107 was struggling to keep up with modern safety innovations.

magazine *Road & Track* still liked it, calling it an 'intriguing blend of the state of the art and the outdated'. It was certainly an effective and still-glamorous blend of both.

It all came to an end in 1989, after the R107 SL had been in production for no less than eighteen years. That was far longer than anyone had envisaged, but it was strong demand that had kept the R107 in production – along with Sindelfingen's preoccupation with more pressing projects such as the S-class and E-class saloons. The R107 had, in fact, been produced for longer than any other model in the history of Mercedes-Benz and that had pushed production up to almost a quarter of a million cars: there were 237,287 R107 SLs, of which the largest seller was the long-running 450 with 66,298 sold, though

both the 560SL and 380SL sold quicker with around 50,000 of each being made in the early eighties. During the second half of that decade the 420SL managed to sell only a paltry 2,148, making it the rarest of the R107s. Another 62,888 were SLC coupés, half of them 450s but fewer than 3,000 with the alloy 5.0-litre engine. In terms of production numbers, at least, the R/C107 had been the most successful SL so far, despite being born into an uncertain world full of new safety regulations and emissions requirements, and having to face fuel crises and economic upheavals. The new SL that would replace the R107 – which was already in production, not in Stuttgart, but at a refurbished factory at Bremen – had an awful lot to live up to.

Handsome as ever, but an anachronism by the time it was finally replaced in 1989, the R107 became an instant classic.

Dark bodywork emphasized the unfashionable chrome trim on the R107. The next generation SL would be very different.

7 R129 –
The Quantum Leap

By the end of the 1970s work had already begun on a successor to the R107 SL, but it would be another decade before the existing SL would be ready to be replaced. In the meantime, there would be discussion after discussion within Daimler-Benz about the type of car that should replace it. Should it be rear-wheel drive and powered by a V8 engine like the R107? Should it be a more technically radical machine, perhaps with a mid-mounted engine – and should that engine be turbocharged, or even based on a completely different concept?

That kind of thinking is an essential part of car design, because the only way to push back the boundaries is to ask challenging questions and develop practical solutions to them. But the idea of making a more radical statement with the next SL by changing the layout of the car or the type of engine that powered it was not simply a flight of fashion: Mercedes-Benz had already proved that it could build cars of that type, so why not put them into production?

Mercedes had developed the mid-engined C111 coupé throughout the 1970s, both as a potential road-going car and as a long-distance record-breaker. When it was first seen, at the Frankfurt motor show in September 1969, it was fitted with a triple-rotor Wankel rotary engine and was later given a four-rotor Wankel. In common with other manufacturers, Mercedes-Benz had extensively tested the rotary engine because of its potential benefits,

particularly its exceptional smoothness compared to a conventional piston engine thanks to its lack of reciprocating components. Wankel units were tried in prototype W113 and R107 SLs, but emissions problems and high fuel-consumption meant that they never progressed into production. Other car makers, notably NSU in Germany and Mazda in Japan, persevered, but in the end only Mazda developed the rotary engine into a workable proposition.

C111, meanwhile, remained nothing more than a research project. Several record-breaking runs, at the Nardo test track in Southern Italy during the latter half of the 1970s, kept the project alive and won Mercedes-Benz speed records in a number of classes – even winning outright world records in diesel-engined form. Though the C111 project was all but over by the end of the decade, it would influence work that was just beginning on a new generation of SLs: the temptation to make the new car a gullwing supercar in the mould of the C111 must have been strong. Mid-engined concepts for the SL were considered, but eventually the radical route was rejected – as was an alternative proposal for a very conventional replacement model. Sharp, angular styles were by then all the rage, but Mercedes-Benz instead steered a conservative course with a car that would blend tradition with innovation: it would be thoroughly modern in everything it did, but at the same time would reflect the heritage of the SL series in its styling and engineering.

The C111 project in the 1970s had shown what future Mercedes-Benz sports cars might be like. The car set numerous long-distance speed records.

The road-going C111 was fitted with a Wankel rotary engine, but the Wankel's fuel consumption and emissions troubles persuaded Mercedes-Benz not to put it into production.

Angular and purposeful, the C111 was right for its time, but never for production.

Like the original SL, the C111 road car was fitted with gullwing doors, but the idea was not carried forward to the new SL.

A Long Time Coming

The long gestation period of the R129 SL finally came to an end at the Geneva show early in 1989. The new SL had taken a back seat during the 1980s because of other major projects, such as the introduction of the compact W201 190 series, the replacement of the long-running W123 saloons and estates by the W124 series, and the development of an important and technically advanced new S-class saloon.

Each one of those projects was an important one for Mercedes-Benz, more important than the creation of a mere sports car, particularly when the existing R107 was still very popular. But the time was coming when the old SL would simply be outclassed, too far behind the times and incapable of the updates and facelifts that had for so long kept it abreast of modern technology and style. A new car was needed and the R129 not only had to embody the latest technology and a mixture of traditional and modern styling, it also had to be a car that would be seen to be as sophisticated and as glamorous as the previous generations of SL had so effortlessly been.

And that was exactly the kind of car that the Geneva showgoers were the first to see in the metal. The SL design team, led by Mercedes-Benz's chief stylist Bruno Sacco, had blended the smooth and efficient styling of the W124 saloon with elements of classic Mercedes models, producing a car that was at once traditional and up-to-date. Aerodynamics played a major role in the shaping of the bodywork, but so too did the desire to make this and all new Mercedes models reflect their best qualities in their appearance. So the new SL looked clean, neat and efficient, and it had tight curves rather than sharp creases to emphasize the strength and solidity that lay beneath the skin.

What it lacked, perhaps, was the elegance of the old car, but that was, if anything, a reflection of what the market wanted and what

rivals were offering. From the front the view was still dominated by horizontal headlamps, now trapezoidal rather than truly rectangular, the wide grille between them carrying an immodestly-sized three-pointed star. As before, the grille was part of the bonnet, but now the styling blended the two into a single unit. Below it there was no longer a substantial, chrome-plated bumper; instead the bumper and the now-essential front air-dam were a continuous polyurethane moulding, to remove the gaps and crannies that would upset the airflow and create aerodynamic drag. Matching side-mouldings protected the car's flanks and unified the styling of the whole car by visually connecting the front and rear bumpers, and at the front they carried air ducts that were reminiscent of those on the Gull-wing 300SL. Some of the colour schemes that were offered were aesthetically dubious, however: a deliberate two-tone effect created by colouring the bumpers and plastic side panels a slightly different hue from the main body tended simply to look like a bad colour match.

To some eyes it was solid and handsome, but others thought the new R129 SL lacked the grace of the old car.

Polyurethane bumpers and side panels protected the car from minor knocks. The two-tone colour schemes were not always successful.

A gentle, but noticeable, nose-down attitude promoted aerodynamic stability and, at the same time, contributed to the more overtly aggressive stance of the new SL. While the long bonnet and short cabin were classic SL trademarks, the R129 now exchanged some of the earlier cars' balance and poise for a clear statement of power and performance.

Innovating in Safety

But the new R129 body was about much more than just striking and modern looks: underneath it was hidden the very latest in engineering. In the eighteen years it had been in production, the previous SL had fallen far behind the state of the art in construction and safety design. The state of the art had more often than not been due to Daimler-Benz developments and the R129 reflected all the latest Sindelfingen safety thinking – along with new ideas that had been born from a desire to make the new SL the safest roadster on the road.

New developments included much greater use of light alloys and high-strength steels than

Testing included an examination of the effects of electromagnetic interference on the car's electronics.

before, while the completely new floorpan on which the car was based had been designed using the latest computer-aided 'finite element analysis' methods. All this meant that the R129

Crash testing was an ever more important part of vehicle engineering and the standards set for the R129 roadster were no less demanding than for the Mercedes saloons.

bodyshell was just 44lb (20kg) heavier than that of the outgoing R107, despite higher equipment levels, an increase of around 30 per cent in torsional stiffness (bringing with it handling and ride benefits) and a much greater degree of secondary safety.

Like the R107 and the W113 before it, the latest SL protected its occupants using a 'safety cell' in the centre of the car, but now the construction of the cell itself and the design of the structures that would protect it were much more sophisticated. At the front, for instance, the chassis members were designed with a varying thickness of metal and given a gradually increasing section, so that they would crush in a controlled way to limit the potentially harmful decelerations suffered by the occupants of the car in a collision. While safety regulations tended to concentrate on impacts square-on to the nose of the car, the safety work that Daimler-Benz had been doing since the 1940s had shown that it was also important to cater for 'offset' collisions, which were more common in real accidents. So the SL was designed with stronger cross-bracing than before, to channel the forces from an offset collision into the full width of the car, employing as much of the structure as possible to deal with the impact.

The inner panels of the doors were designed to act as stiff, stable structures that fed loads into the opposite end of the safety cell from the collision, while themselves resisting any tendency to crush – so preserving the safety cell. They also resisted side impacts, overlapping the sills to feed impact loads into a substantial cross-brace under the seats.

The seats themselves played an innovative

safety role. One of the safety problems with coupés and convertibles is that there is often no substantial B-pillar where seat belts can be mounted, or that the long doors push the pillar too far back. On the SEC coupés the seat belts were so far back they had to be handed forward to the driver and passenger by a robotic arm, but now the new SL solved the problem in an entirely new way. Instead of the belts being mounted on the body, they were carried on the seat frame, which itself was made up from high-strength, lightweight magnesium castings. The top mounting of the belt and the integral head restraint adjusted up and down together, so that the belt was always at the right height for the wearer. Another important element of the seat design, which incorporated twenty patents for its detail features, was the automatic locking mechanism, which ensured the seat was always correctly positioned after it had been tipped forward for access to the rear of the cabin.

One safety innovation garnered more column inches than any other, however, and that was the new SL's automatic roll-over bar. Mercedes was aiming at a higher standard of roll-over protection than before, high enough to mean that the A-pillars (despite internal high-strength steel tubes) could not be expected to carry the impact loads alone. A conventional fixed roll-bar spoiled the lines of the car, despite dozens of different attempts to make it look like it belonged. A retractable roll-bar was the answer: normally it sat horizontally behind the rear seat, forming a padded inner edge of the cockpit surround. But when sensors detected that the car was about to roll, the spring-loaded bar flipped up in less than a third of a second to protect the occupants. At the same time the system locked the seat belts in position and unlocked the doors so that they would be easy to open from inside or out when the car came to rest.

The flip-up roll bar was designed to operate just as effectively whether the car was being driven with the soft top down or up, or

The SL was now offered with an aluminium hard-top, which was lighter than before, but still a heavy item to lift and difficult to store when not in use. The automatic roll-bar worked whether or not the top was in place.

The seats were an important part of the SL's occupant protection system, carrying the seat-belt mountings.

The seats and their integral seat belts were proven in laboratory tests using crash-test dummies scientifically designed to mimic the human body.

with a hard top fitted. The hard top had been improved by making it substantially of aluminium alloy, reducing its weight to a more manageable, if still rather heavy, 75lb (34kg). The soft-top roof was now a much more elaborate affair than on the previous SL, with electro-hydraulic operation, and unlike many other power-operated roofs there were no manual locks or levers to operate: the driver just held down a button to raise or lower the roof. Just to prove that they had thought of everything, Mercedes also supplied a folding 'windbreak' made of black plastic mesh, which could be erected behind the front-seat passengers to keep the cockpit gust-free when the car was driven with the roof down.

Chassis Superiority

While the SL was designed to perform well in an impact, the Mercedes way had always been to engineer a chassis that gave the driver a good chance of avoiding a collision in the first place. The R129 received the latest low-profile tyres, still in the conservative widths

The seat belts were arranged to move up and down with the head restraints, so that the belt was always at the right height for the occupant.

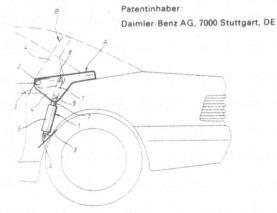

BUNDESREPUBLIK DEUTSCHLAND

DEUTSCHES PATENTAMT

Patentschrift
DE 37 32 562 C 1

Aktenzeichen:	P 37 32 562.0-21
Anmeldetag:	26. 9. 87
Offenlegungstag:	—
Veröffentlichungstag der Patenterteilung:	24. 11. 88

innerhalb von 3 Monaten nach Veröffentlichung der Erteilung kann Einspruch erhoben werden

Patentinhaber:
Daimler-Benz AG, 7000 Stuttgart, DE

Antriebsvorrichtung für einen Überrollbügel für Kraftwagen

Of all the SL's safety features, the patented flip-up roll-over bar gained the most publicity.

Normally stowed horizontally, the automatic roll-over bar sprang up automatically in a third of a second if the system detected the car was about to roll. In this test the bar had already locked in place by the time the SL had rolled onto its side.

typical of Mercedes but now 55-series tyres on bigger 16in alloy wheels, which allowed larger brake-discs to be fitted inside them at the front. ABS anti-lock braking was standard and the sensors that provided wheel-speed information to the ABS computer were also used to sense wheel spin during acceleration by comparing the speed of the driven wheels with that of the undriven front wheels. Engine output was curbed automatically to quell the wheel spin and, in extreme cases, the system applied the brake on the spinning wheel.

The suspension was derived from the W201 and W124, which meant it was different in concept at both ends from the outgoing SL. At the back there was a 'multi-link' layout, with five separate suspension arms on each side and geometry which controlled tail-lift under braking and squat under acceleration. As was the modern way, the suspension bushes

were carefully tuned to improve handling: the bushes in the lower track control-arms were compliant enough to allow the outside rear wheel to toe-in slightly while cornering, promoting gentle, stabilizing understeer. A self-levelling system was also incorporated to keep the car level when fully loaded.

At the front the old car's double wishbone layout, fundamentally the same as that on the 190SL of the mid-fifties, was now replaced by a strut-type suspension – with separate mounting points for the gas-filled damper and the suspension spring rather than the more conventional concentric mounting. Effectively, a strut-type suspension is a double-wishbone with a top wishbone of zero length; struts share many of the advantages of wishbones, but are lighter and take up less space at the front of the car. That is why they are popular on modern front-drive cars with transverse engines, which necessarily

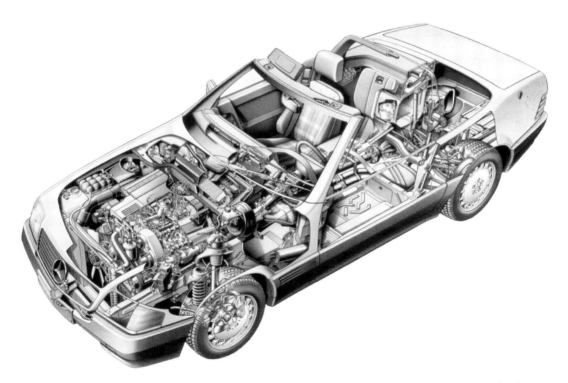

Technologically advanced, the R129 offered much higher levels of performance and occupant safety than the model it replaced.

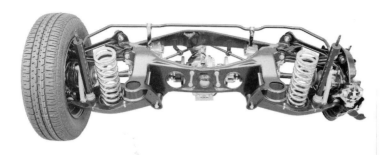

'Multi-link' rear suspension had been introduced on the Mercedes saloons in the 1980s. A development of this system was used on the R129.

need a lot of space between the suspension turrets. The SL, too, needed more space in its engine bay – to accommodate engines which had, in some cases, grown bulkier.

Four-Valve Technology

There was a choice of three engines in the new SL. At the bottom of the range sat the 300SL, powered by a mildly modified version of the M193 3.0-litre six that had been seen in the R107. Above that sat a 300SL-24, still with a 3.0-litre in-line six but now the M104 unit, with four valves per cylinder operated by twin overhead camshafts. Four-valve heads were another modern development that R107 had missed out on: just about every self-respecting performance car of the 1990s would wear a four-valve cylinder head on its engine. Greater airflow was one benefit, because two small inlet valves could flow more air than one large one, an equally important gain being the cleaner, more efficient combustion encouraged by the faster airflow through the small valves, even at part throttle.

But the 24-valve engine had another important trick up its sleeve: variable inlet-valve timing. For maximum power at high speeds there needs to be a large amount of valve overlap, the period where the intake and exhaust valves are open at the same time. As the exhaust gas rushes out, it leaves a partial vacuum behind in the combustion chamber, which can help suck in air/fuel mixture – but only if the intake valves are open. At low engine speeds a large amount of overlap allows unburnt fuel to escape through the open exhaust valves, hurting fuel economy and emissions performance. Conventionally, valve timing is a compromise between the requirements of low and high engine speeds, but variable valve timing offers the best of both worlds. Mercedes employed an electro-hydraulic system to rotate the intake camshaft relative to its drive gear, under control of the engine management system. As the engine speed rose the intake cam was progressively advanced to increase overlap, improving mid-range torque and top-end power. As a result the 24-valve engine developed 231bhp, over 40bhp more than the 12-valve engine in the 300SL. Both models were available with five-speed manual or four-speed automatic gearboxes but, in addition, the 300SL-24 could be ordered with a five-speed automatic gearbox with an overdrive top gear. To take advantage of the higher gearing of the five-speed auto it came with a lower final-drive ratio, so acceleration was swifter but cruising was still quiet and relatively economical.

Naturally a V8 engine was set to power the top models in the R129 range – and the V8 was bulkier than before because it, too, now employed four-valve cylinder heads and twin overhead camshafts on each bank of cylinders. Like the 300SL-24's six-cylinder engine, the

R129 In-Line Six

Chassis and body	Unitary steel body
Engine	Front engine, longitudinal, inclined 15 degrees to the right
Designation	300SL: M103 E30
	300SL-24: M104 E30/2
	SL280: M104 E28
	SL320: M104 E32
Block material	Aluminium alloy
Head material	Aluminium alloy
Cylinders	300SL/300SL-24/SL280/SL320: 6 in-line;
Cooling	Water
Lubrication	Wet sump
Bore × stroke	300SL/300SL-24: 88.5 × 80.2mm
	SL280: 89.9 × 73.5mm
	SL320: 89.9 × 84mm
Capacity	300SL/300SL-24: 2960cc
	SL280: 2799cc
	SL320: 3199cc
Main bearings	300SL/300SL-24/SL280/SL320: 7
Valves/operation	300SL: Single chain-driven overhead camshaft, twelve valves operated by rockers
	300SL-24/SL280: Twin chain-driven overhead camshafts, twenty-four valves, variable intake cam timing
Compression ratio	300SL: 9.2:1
	300SL-24/SL280/SL320: 10.0:1
Fuel system	Bosch fuel injection
Maximum power	300SL: 190bhp @ 5,700rpm
	300SL-24: 231bhp @ 6,300rpm
	SL280: 193bhp @ 5,500rpm
	SL320: 231bhp @ 5,600rpm
Maximum torque	300SL: 192lb ft @ 4,500rpm
	300SL-24: 201lb ft @ 4,600rpm
	SL280: 199lb ft @ 3,750rpm
	SL320: 232lb ft @ 3,750rpm
Transmission	Rear-wheel drive
	300SL/300SL-24/SL280: Five-speed manual gearbox, four-speed automatic optional
	300SL-24/SL280: Five-speed automatic optional from 1989
	SL320: Five-speed automatic standard
Type	Five-speed manual, 300SL/SL280
Gear ratios (1-2-3-4-5-R)	3.86-2.18-1.38-1.00-0.80-4.22
Clutch	Dry single-plate
Final-drive ratio	3.92:1 (3.89:1 from June 1996)
Type	Five-speed manual, 300SL-24
Gear ratios (1-2-3-4-5-R)	4.15-2.52-1.69-1.24-1.00-4.15
Clutch	Dry single-plate
Final-drive ratio	3.46:1
Type	Four-speed automatic, optional on 300SL/300SL-24
Gear ratios (1-2-3-4-R)	3.87-2.25-1.44-1.00-5.59
Coupling	Torque converter

R129 In-Line Six *continued*

Final-drive ratio	300SL: 3.29:1; 300SL-24: 3.46:1
Type	Four-speed automatic, optional on SL280
Gear ratios (1-2-3-4-R)	4.25–2.41–1.49–1.00–5.67
Coupling	Torque converter
Final-drive ratio	3.27:1
Type	Five-speed automatic, optional on 300SL-24/SL280 from 1989, standard on SL320 up to August 1995
Gear ratios (1-2-3-4-5-R)	3.87–2.25–1.44–1.00–0.75–5.59
Coupling	Torque converter
Final-drive ratio	3.69:1 (3.67:1 from June 1996)
Type	Five-speed automatic, standard on SL320 from September 1995
Gear ratios (1-2-3-4-5-R)	3.93–2.41–1.49–1.00–0.83–3.10
Coupling	Torque converter
Final-drive ratio	3.45:1

Suspension and steering

Front	Lower wishbone and coil-spring strut, anti-roll bar
Rear	Multi-link, coil springs, telescopic dampers, anti-roll bar
Steering	Recirculating ball with power assistance
Wheels	8J × 16 light-alloy wheels
Tyres	Radial, 225/55ZR16
Brakes	Hydraulically operated dual-circuit disc brakes, ventilated at front. Anti-lock system standard. Brake Assist from December 1996

Dimensions

Length	176in (4,470mm)
Width	71.3in (1,811mm)
Height	51.3in (1,303mm)
Track – front	60.4in (1,534mm)
Track – rear	60in (1,524mm)
Wheelbase	99.0in (2,515mm)
Unladen weight	3,630–4,070lb (1,650–1,850kg)
Fuel tank capacity	17.6gal (80ltr)

Performance

Top speed	300SL: 142mph (228km/h)
	300SL-24: 146mph (235km/h)
	SL280: 140mph (225km/h)
	SL320: 149mph (240km/h)
Acceleration	0–62mph (100km/h)
	300SL: 9.3sec
	300SL-24: 8.4sec
	SL280: 9.9sec
	SL320: 8.4sec

V8 also incorporated variable intake-valve timing. Based on the alloy-blocked V8 from the previous 500SL, the new engine kept its 96.5mm bore and 85mm stroke for a capacity of 4973cc, but the crankcase, crankshaft and connecting rods had all been revised. It now developed 326bhp at 5,500rpm – up from the 223bhp of the 16-valve V8 in its final, catalyst-equipped form. The 0–60mph (97km/h) time dropped from nearly eight seconds for the old car to a fraction over six seconds, but the improvement in top speed was less substantial than it might have been: the old 500SL was all out at 134mph (215km/h), while the new one had a speed limiter built into its engine man-agement system, which would not allow it to exceed 155mph (250km/h).

Predictably the press reaction to the new SL was very positive, though some testers found things to criticize while still acknowl-edging the overall competence and impres-siveness of the machine. Some questioned whether all the 'electrickery' was really nec-essary, whether the electric roof was really any better than the easy-to-use manual roof of the previous SL, whether the fancy flip-up roll bar and the interfering traction control were anything more than just gimmicks to

Comfort and luxury were the watchwords for the new SL interior. Wood covered the centre console and leather trim was available.

lure punters into the showroom. There were also some who struggled with the new styling of the SL, applauding its aerodynamic virtues but missing the elegance and character of the old car. The seats were still too firm, but there were plaudits for the choice this time round of a smaller steering wheel.

There was disquiet in some quarters about the brakes not being up to much, but gener-ally few people had anything less than praise for the chassis. The handling was accom-plished, the ride cosseting and, for the large and heavy car the SL proved to be, surefooted and swift. Everyone agreed that Mercedes had achieved an enormous amount with the new SL, bringing it up to date with the latest in technology and a huge stride forward in sec-ondary safety.

Buyers agreed with the positive press verdict and flocked to Mercedes-Benz showrooms to place their orders, despite prices that, in Britain, began at £42,130 and rose to a minimum of £58,045 for the 500SL (and often more once optional extras were added). With annual production at Bremen limited to 20,000 there was soon a waiting list stretching to several years. But this was the age of the speculator, with values of classic cars rising beyond all previous records and limited-run new cars being created specially for a new breed of collector. Soon those lucky enough to get their hands on a new SL were able to sell it on at a fat profit, but the bubble quickly burst. Worries on the world's stock markets saw the speculators scurry back to look after their other investments and soon something approaching order was restored.

Twelve Cylinders

A new SL model appeared three and a half years later. The 600SL was powered by the V12 engine that had already been developed for use in the S-class saloon – not that there was much wrong with the Mercedes V8s, but the marketing men wanted a V12 to match those on offer from Jaguar and, more importantly, BMW. What they got was a 5987cc V12 with four valves per cylinder, originally developing a little over 400bhp – considerably more than the BMW V12, which generated 300bhp from 4988cc. By the time the long and wide Mercedes V12 had been insinuated into the nose of the SL it had lost a little power, in deference to Germany's environmental lobby, enrichment of the air/fuel mixture at full throttle having been removed to improve fuel economy and reduce emissions. Even so there was a still considerable 394bhp at 5,200rpm and, with a torque peak of no less than 420lb ft, it hardly needed a gearbox at all, but it was given a four-speed auto as standard.

Journalists who drove it were impressed by the V12 SL's performance, refinement and safety, and also by the way such a big, heavy car could be so responsive and surefooted on the road. They also noted that much the same things could be said about the lesser models and wondered quite what the 600SL was for. In *CAR*, Georg Kacher suggested that the V12 was 'the answer to a question nobody asked' and urged readers to buy a 500SL instead. But most accepted that for anyone

Minor interior changes throughout the R129 production were aimed at improved appearance and convenience.

with almost £97,000 to spend on a car the 600SL was just about the best combination of speed, comfort and security that it was possible to buy.

New Names, New Engines

Less than a year later, in June 1993, Mercedes-Benz introduced a new nomenclature for all its cars. The old system of a number (usually) representing the engine capacity followed by a sequence of letters indicating the type of car was reversed so that the letters preceded the

AMG's 'ultimate SLs' were based on both the V8 and V12 cars.

R129 V8 and V12	
Chassis and body	Unitary steel body
Engine	Front engine, longitudinal
Designation	500SL/SL500 (until May 1998): M119 E50
	SL500 from June 1988: M113 E50
	600SL/SL600: M120 E60
Block material	Aluminium alloy
Head material	Aluminium alloy
Cylinders	500SL/SL500: V8
	600SL/SL600: V12
Cooling	Water
Lubrication	Wet sump
Bore × stroke	500SL/SL500 (M119): 96.5 × 85mm
	SL500 (M113): 97.0 × 84.0mm
	600SL/SL600: 89.0 × 80.2mm
Capacity	500SL/SL500 (M119): 4973cc
	SL500: (M113): 4966cc
	600SL/SL600: 5987cc
Main bearings	500SL: 5
	600SL/SL600: 7
Valves/operation	Twin chain-driven overhead camshafts per cylinder bank
	500SL/SL500 (M119): 32 valves
	SL500 (M113): 24 valves (two intake, one exhaust)
	600SL/SL600: 48 valves
Compression ratio	10.0:1
Fuel system	Bosch fuel injection
Maximum power	500SL/SL500 (M119): 326bhp @ 5,500rpm (320bhp @ 5,600rpm from September 1992)
	SL500 (M113): 306bhp @ 5,600rpm
	600SL/SL600: 394bhp @ 5,200rpm
Maximum torque	500SL/SL500 (M119): 332lb ft @ 4,000rpm (347lb ft @ 3,900rpm from September 1992)
	SL500 (M113): 339lb ft @ 2,700–4,250rpm
	600SL/SL600: 420lb ft @ 3,800rpm
Transmission	Rear-wheel drive. Four-speed automatic standard, five-speed automatic standard from 1996
Type	Four-speed automatic
Gear ratios (1-2-3-4-R)	3.87-2.25-1.44-1.00-5.59
Coupling	Torque converter
Final-drive ratio	2.65:1
Type	Five-speed automatic, standard on SL500 and SL600 from September 1996
Gear ratios (1-2-3-4-5-R)	3.59-2.19-1.41-1.00-0.83-3.16
Coupling	Torque converter
Final-drive ratio	2.65:1
Suspension and steering	
Front	Lower wishbone and strut, anti-roll bar
	500SL: coil springs
	600SL: hydropneumatic spring struts

R129 V8 and V12 *continued*	
Rear	Multi-link, telescopic dampers, anti-roll bar
	500SL: coil springs
	600SL: hydropneumatic spring struts
Steering	Recirculating ball with power assistance
Wheels	8J × 16 light-alloy wheels (8.25J × 17 from 1998)
Tyres	Radial, 225/55ZR16 (245/45R17 from 1998)
Brakes	Hydraulically operated dual-circuit disc brakes, ventilated at front. Anti-lock system standard. Brake Assist standard from December 1996
Dimensions	
Length	176in (4,470mm)
Width	71.3in (1,811mm)
Height	51.3in (1,303mm)
Track – front	60.4in (1,534mm)
Track – rear	60in (1,524mm)
Wheelbase	99.0in (2,515mm)
Unladen weight	3,902–4,519lb (1,770–2,050kg)
Fuel tank capacity	17.6gal (80ltr)
Performance	
Top speed	Electronically limited to 155mph (250km/h)
Acceleration	0–62mph (100km/h)
	500SL/SL500: 6.2sec (6.5sec from September 1992)
	600SL/SL600: 6.1sec

numbers and, at the same time, the letter system was simplified. What was once a 600SEL long-wheelbase saloon, for instance, was now just badged S600, while the corresponding V12 SL was now the SL600.

At the same time the 3.0-litre six-cylinder engines in the 300SL and 300SL-24 were dropped. In their place came two new versions of the four-valve M104 straight-six engine that had been in the 300SL-24, but now in 2.8-litre and 3.2-litre capacities. The smaller unit, in the SL280, had already been in use in the mid-size saloon – now known as the 'E-class' – and the big S-class, and generated slightly better power and torque figures, but without any fuel consumption penalty compared to the two-valve M103 engine. The new SL320 had the same power output as the old 300SL-24, but achieved maximum power

at lower revs and generated more torque throughout the rev-range or improved drive-ability now all SL models except the 'entry level' SL280 were fitted as standard with automatic transmissions.

At the other end of the scale it was now possible to buy a V8-engined SL with almost as much power as the V12, thanks to Mercedes tuner AMG. The SL500's V8 was expanded both in bore and stroke for a capacity of 5956cc (just 31cc behind the V12) and the AMG engine's maximum power and torque figures were very close to the V12 at 381bhp (6bhp down) and 428lb ft (7lb ft up). The AMG car shaved nearly a second from the standard SL500 0–62mph (100km/h) time, but was still electronically limited to 155mph (250km/h) like other high-performance cars from German manufacturers.

AMG: Modifying Mercedes

Hans-Werner Aufrecht and Erhard Melcher founded AMG (the initials stand for Aufrecht, Melcher and Aufrecht's birthplace, Grobaspach) in 1967. The company built racing engines and then prepared racing cars, and in 1971 an AMG-prepared Mercedes-Benz 300SEL 6.3 (with a big-bore 6.8-litre engine) finished second in the Spa 24-hour race, winning its class. Since then the company has clocked up numerous victories in touring car and GT racing, and has also become widely respected as a tuner of Mercedes road cars.

Originally based in an old mill in the German town of Burgstall, AMG moved to Affalterbach, just a few kilometres to the north-east of Stuttgart, in 1978. Following a formal agreement with Daimler-Benz in 1990, AMG cars could be sold through Mercedes dealers and that led to a period of rapid expansion for the company. In 1999 Daimler-Benz took over as majority shareholder and, since then, the new Mercedes-AMG GmbH has been developing high-performance models in parallel with the more mainstream products being designed at Sindelfingen.

In the DaimlerChrysler era AMG's own products have ranged from relatively high-volume models such as the C32 AMG to niche products like the V12-engined SL73 AMG and even one-off modifications for particularly demanding (and well-heeled) customers. Mercedes-AMG can call upon the DaimlerChrysler group's engineering and test facilities when it needs to, and these days AMG models are planned into new model programmes from the start – unlike AMG's independent years, when Aufrecht would not even see new Mercedes models until their public announcement.

But even now Affalterbach is regarded as a separate entity, with responsibility for its own product development and its own marketing. In theory this gives it the flexibility and rapid response of a small company – and the clout of big one.

Both the V8 and V12 engines were revised in 1995, with an individual coil for each spark plug and new engine management systems on both engines, while the V8 received more far-reaching modifications with a new crankshaft, revised valve timing and lighter pistons. Both SL500 and SL600 were also fitted with a new design of five-speed automatic transmission, which was lighter and more efficient than the old design and constantly exchanged information with the engine management system to ensure gearchanges were smooth and well-timed. As a result, the fuel consumption of both the V8 and V12 SLs improved by around 10 per cent, without any noticeable effect on performance.

The running gear had received attention, too. From the start, the SL had been available with ADS, an adaptive damping system that could adjust the damper settings to suit load and road conditions and also automatically lowered the car slightly at high speed to reduce wind resistance. Now two more technical advances were added to the roster of technical gadgets that could be specified on the SL. ESP, the Electronic Stability Programme, recognized when the car was starting to slide in a corner and helped out the driver by applying the brakes on one or more wheels. The BAS 'Brake Assist' system was another innovation, developed after safety research showed that many drivers failed to apply the brakes hard enough in an emergency situation. BAS was designed to recognize when the driver was braking in an emergency and automatically apply full braking pressure to all four brakes.

Turin Debut

There had been some minor styling updates and interior changes during 1995, and a new hard top with a glass roof and internal sunblind had been made available. At the 1998 Turin show another round of exterior revisions was revealed, along with yet another set of new engines for the SL range.

These new engines – a pair of V6s replacing the in-line M104 engines and a new V8 – had three valves in each combustion chamber, with two small inlet-valves and a single, larger

SLK: the 190SL Reborn

The Mazda MX-5 started it all. By the mid-1980s it had seemed that the affordable roadster was dead, killed off by ever more stringent safety legislation and a whole new generation of sophisticated, effective hot hatchbacks. But the MX-5 showed that there was still life in the roadster concept and it was quickly followed by numerous other open sports cars that aimed at a market significantly below the Mercedes SLs.

The SLK returned Mercedes-Benz to the sub-SL segment that had been occupied by the 190SL in the 1950s.

The Sindelfingen response was to offer a more modestly priced roadster of its own, the SLK – the designation reviving memories of the pre-war SSK, the K in both cases standing for *kurz*, German for 'short'. It first appeared as a concept at the Turin show in 1994 and then a modified version was seen at Paris in October the same year, unveiling one of the features that would go on to make the SLK famous: the 'Vario' roof.

Designed so the driver can switch between convertible and true hard-top motoring at the push of a button, the Vario roof is made of steel and can be folded away into the boot using an electro-hydraulic system, the whole procedure taking just twenty-five seconds. With the roof down, two fixed roll-hoops behind the seats are revealed.

The original engine range included a 2.0-litre in-line four already used in the C-class and E-class, a supercharged 2.0-litre for Italy, Portugal and Greece, and a supercharged 2.3-litre four shared with the C230 Kompressor. In 2000 a 3.2-litre V6 was added and, for those who never thought enough was enough, there was an SLK32 AMG with 354bhp and 332lb ft of torque. By then Daimler-Benz had merged with the Chrysler Corporation to create Daimler-Chrysler and one of the results of the integration of the two companies was Chrysler's Crossfire coupé, based on the SLK platform.

Some commentators suggested that the SLK, for all its looks and safety and build quality, did not feel as special to drive as some competitors, like Audi's TT or Porsche's Boxster. But like the 190SL almost half a century earlier, the SLK was aimed at a particular niche in the market – and it provided just what its customers wanted.

exhaust-valve. That left room for twin spark plugs, which helped to ensure that no unburnt fuel left the cylinders. As a result the new engines were more economical and had better emissions performance than the units they replaced. As before, there was an SL280, now with a 204bhp version of the M112 V6, and a 224bhp SL320. The SL500 now had the M113 V8 engine developing 306bhp (14bhp less than the outgoing V8), and at the top of the range there was still the V12 SL600, now with 394bhp. AMG's 6.0-litre version of the old V8 was discontinued, but in 1999 (with

DaimlerChrysler now a majority shareholder) AMG introduced a pair of high-performance SLs: first an SL73 AMG with a 7291cc 525bhp V12 and then a slightly more restrained 5439cc 354bhp V8 SL55 AMG.

The styling did a good job of minimizing the unfashionable bulk that had pervaded Mercedes-Benz products of the early 1990s – the greatest criticism being levelled at the S-class saloon, which compounded the problem of being a vast and profligate motor car in an environmentally-conscious age by *looking* like a vast and profligate motor car. The SL, too,

SLK230 Kompressor

Chassis and body	Unitary steel body
Engine	Front engine, longitudinal
Designation	M111 E23
Block material	Aluminium alloy
Head material	Aluminium alloy
Cylinders	4 in-line
Cooling	Water
Lubrication	Wet sump
Bore × stroke	90.9 × 88.4
Capacity	2295cc
Main bearings	5
Valves/operation	Twin chain-driven overhead camshafts, variable intake valve timing, 16 valves
Compression ratio	8.8:1
Fuel system	Bosch ME engine management, supercharger with charge-air cooling
Maximum power	193bhp @ 5,300rpm
Maximum torque	206lb ft @ 2,500–4,800rpm
Transmission	Rear-wheel drive. Five-speed manual gearbox, five-speed automatic optional
Type	Five-speed manual
Gear ratios (1-2-3-4-5-R)	3.86-2.18-1.38-1.00-0.80-4.22
Clutch	Dry single-plate
Final-drive ratio	3.46:1
Type	Five-speed automatic, optional
Gear ratios (1-2-3-4-R)	3.93-2.41-1.49-1.00-0.83-3.10
Coupling	Torque converter with lock-up clutch
Final-drive ratio	3.27:1
Suspension and steering	
Front	Double wishbone, coil-spring, telescopic dampers and anti-roll bar
Rear	Multi-link, coil springs, telescopic dampers
Steering	Recirculating ball with power assistance
Wheels	Light-alloy wheels 7J × 16 front, 8J × 16 rear
Tyres	Radial, 205/55R16V front, 225/50R16V rear
Brakes	Hydraulically operated dual-circuit disc brakes, ventilated at front. Anti-lock system standard. Brake Assist standard from 1997
Dimensions	
Length	157.3in (3,995mm)
Width	67.5in (1,715mm)
Height	50.6in (1,285mm)
Track – front	58.6in (1,488mm)
Track – rear	58.5in (1,486mm)
Wheelbase	94.5in (2,400mm)
Unladen weight	1,325kg
Fuel tank capacity	11.6gal (53ltr)
Performance	
Top speed	143mph (231km/h)
Acceleration	0–62mph (100km/h) 7.4sec

Note that other SLK models are available: SLK200, SLK200 Kompressor, SLK320, SLK32 AMG

R129 V6

Chassis and body	Unitary steel body
Engine	Front engine, longitudinal
Designation	SL280: M112 E28
	SL320: M112 E32
Block material	Aluminium alloy
Head material	Aluminium alloy
Cylinders	V6
Cooling	Water
Lubrication	Wet sump
Bore × stroke	SL280: 89.9 × 73.5mm
	SL320 (M104): 89.9 × 84mm
Capacity	SL280: 2799cc
	SL320: 3199cc
Main bearings	4
Valves/operation	Twin chain-driven overhead camshafts per bank, eighteen valves (two intake and one exhaust)
Compression ratio	10.0:1
Fuel system	Bosch fuel injection
Maximum power	SL280: 204bhp @ 5,700rpm
	SL320: 224bhp @ 5,600rpm
Maximum torque	SL280: 199lb ft @ 3,000–5,000rpm
	SL320: 232lb ft @ 3,000–4,800rpm
Transmission	Rear-wheel drive. Five-speed manual gearbox, five-speed automatic optional (standard on SL320)
Type	Five-speed manual, 300SL/SL280
Gear ratios (1-2-3-4-5-R)	3.86-2.18-1.38-1.00-0.80-4.22
Clutch	Dry single-plate
Final-drive ratio	3.92:1
Type	Five-speed automatic, optional on SL280
Gear ratios (1-2-3-4-5-R)	3.87-2.25-1.44-1.00-0.75-5.59
Coupling	Torque converter
Final-drive ratio	3.69:1
Type	Five-speed automatic, standard on SL320
Gear ratios (1-2-3-4-5-R)	3.93-2.41-1.49-1.00-0.83-3.10
Coupling	Torque converter
Final-drive ratio	3.45:1
Suspension and steering	
Front	Lower wishbone and coil-spring strut, anti-roll bar
Rear	Multi-link, coil springs, telescopic dampers, anti-roll bar
Steering	Recirculating ball with power assistance
Wheels	8.25J × 17 light-alloy wheels
Tyres	Radial, 245/45ZR17
Brakes	Hydraulically operated dual-circuit disc brakes, ventilated at front. Anti-lock system standard. Brake Assist
Dimensions	
Length	177in (4,496mm)
Width	71.3in (1,811mm)
Height	51.3in (1,303mm)
Track – front	60.4in (1,534mm)
Track – rear	60in (1,524mm)
Wheelbase	99.0in (2,515mm)
Unladen weight	3,990–4,034lb (1,810–1,830kg)
Fuel tank capacity	17.6gal (80ltr)
Performance	
Top speed	SL280: 142mph (228km/h)
	SL320: 148mph (238km/h)
Acceleration	0–62mph (100km/h)
	SL280: 9.5sec
	SL320: 8.4sec

The special edition cars like the 'Silver Arrow' received even more opulent interiors.

A glass roof with an internal sunblind was a new option from 1995.

Towards the end of its run the R129 was given a minor facelift to lighten its appearance. This is one of the final 'Silver Arrow' special edition cars.

had always looked chunky and tough rather than lithe and efficient, whatever the truth about the car may have been. Now a restyled rear end with single-colour tail lights sought to make the SL's shape simpler and more elegant, while curvaceous SLK-style mirrors helped lighten the shape and emphasize its performance rather than its solidity.

The styling changes were relatively minor, but then all they were intended to do was to freshen up the appearance of the now decade-old SL in the face of new rivals from Porsche, BMW, Jaguar, Aston Martin and others. A major rework was not necessary because the R129, unlike the R107 before it, was not being expected to soldier on for years to come.

In fact, work on its successor was already far advanced and the debut of a whole new SL was just around the corner.

More than 200,000 units had been built by the time R129 production ended in the summer of 2001, by which time total 'SL-class' production since 1952 stood at just under half a million. The SL family had proved to be one of Mercedes-Benz's most successful lines and one of the most sought-after families of sports cars from any manufacturer since the beginning of the motor industry. Now a new generation was ready to carry the SLs into a new millennium.

Built in Bremen

The R129 may have had some styling details that harked back to past models, but in many ways it was a new departure. It was even built in a different place.

Until 1989 all the SL models had been built in Stuttgart, the production models coming off the lines between S-class and mid-size saloons, but production of the R129 was carried out at Daimler-Benz's Bremen plant. Owned by Borgward until 1961, the Bremen factory was then used by commercial vehicle builders Hanomag and Hanomag-Henschel, before it became the site for Mercedes-Benz van production in 1974. Car production began there with the W123 estate cars in 1978. Major investment was made in the Bremen plant in 1982 with the construction of an additional production facility for the W201 (190 series) saloon, which was also built on a parallel production line at Sindelfingen.

R129 production began at Bremen in 1989, slightly overlapping with the end of R107 SL production at Sindelfingen. Since then all SLs have been made at Bremen, which also houses production lines for the SLK roadster.

Previous SL models were built in Stuttgart but, for the R129 production, moved to the Bremen factory, which had originally been used by Borgward.

8   SLs for a New Millennium

When Mercedes-Benz launched the R230 SL in Hamburg in the summer of 2001, it was instantly apparent where they had got their styling ideas. The outgoing R129 SL had incorporated some subtle styling elements, which were a nod to Mercedes models of the past, but the R230 went a step further: looking round the car you could easily see the influence of the legendary 300SL in the new car's design. Manufacturers the world over were realizing that evoking memories of past glories was a short-cut to a glamorous image and were falling all over themselves to produce 'retro' shapes.

At the same time, the design of the new SL managed to look far more dynamic and purposeful than the R129. A nose-down appearance had been a strong theme in the original set of ideas for the car, drawn up by ten designers, whose draft proposals were assessed in January 1996. From there the ideas had been developed using two very different methods: a computer-controlled virtual world was used to examine the new car from every angle, while quarter-scale models provided a real-world input into the styling. The result was a design that looked powerful and at the same time controlled, with a hint of a predatory animal coiled ready to pounce, but there was also a feeling of solidity and balance – and those were just the kind of attributes the stylists wanted the new model to be imbued with.

The final design was given the green light by the Board of Management on 16 June 1997. While some of the styling elements were a deliberate throwback to earlier models and in particular to the 300SL, like the side vents with their horizontal chrome trim-strips, there were others that recalled the past almost accidentally. For the first time in nearly half a century the SL had something approaching circular headlamps, which were part of the four-eyed Mercedes family face that had first been seen on the 1995 E-class. In its SL incarnation, however, the four-lamp front end was much more dynamic, with the lamps fused together and the nose strongly swept back both in the horizontal and vertical planes. It gave the SL a more penetrating snout, which looked lower, lighter and altogether fresher than the R129 and contributed to a much-improved drag coefficient of 0.29.

Unlike the slab-sided R129, the new SL had a feature line extending backwards from the bottom of the air vent to the rear wheel-arch and then picking up the line of the rear bumper to tie the whole car together visually. This cohesiveness was emphasized by another, subtler, crease emerging from the curves above each front wheel-arch and forming a shoulder line at the top of the door, gradually rising to give the rear arches a muscular shape and then blending into the high tail. There, the familiar Mercedes rear lights had been slashed diagonally by the boot lid, helping to lighten the appearance of the tail.

Making the new body look lighter was one thing, but Mercedes also took steps to make sure it *was* lighter. Aluminium alloys were used

Early styling proposals for the new SL varied from bland to radical. Elements recalling the 1950s 300SL dominated the final design.

Computers did aid the process, allowing design changes to be swiftly assessed.

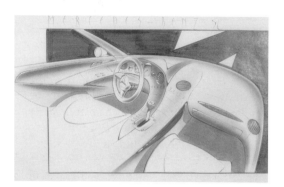

Interior styling was also carefully considered, to provide an attractive and welcoming environment.

Though this was the age of computers, designers still often put down their ideas on paper.

These quarter-scale models, showing alternative design proposals, gave a real-world input into the design process.

A 'virtual reality' projection of the proposed SL shape helped designers to assess the new car from every angle. The final shape was decided in June 1997.

Extensive aerodynamic development gave the R230 a much lower drag coefficient than its predecessor.

The new face of the SL had four headlamps, fused together in pairs. The very latest xenon lamp technology was incorporated.

for much of the outer bodywork, including the bonnet, front wings and boot lid, and Mercedes were particularly proud of their huge alloy bonnet structure, which was 33lb (15kg) lighter than a steel one. The whole shell weighed the same as that of the R129, even thought it was substantially stiffer than before thanks to even wider use of high-strength steels, which now made up a third of the body, to the benefit of ride, handling, safety and refinement.

Roadster, or Coupé?

The roof was another new innovation in the SL line, though it had already been proven in the smaller SLK. Ever since 1957, the SL had been essentially a convertible-roofed roadster with an optional, removable, hard top. But now the SL incorporated the folding 'Vario roof', which meant it could be turned from a full convertible to a snug saloon in seconds, at the press of a button on the centre console. A new 'intelligent' folding mechanism folded the aluminium roof back into the top part of the boot in just sixteen seconds (quicker than the SLK, which took twenty-five seconds) and ensured that the roof elements took up as little space as possible in the boot. As if to prove that they had thought of everything, Mercedes incorporated an 'Easy pack' function, which raised the stowed roof slightly at the press of a button, to make it easier to load luggage into the boot space underneath. When the roof was closed, the boot was usefully larger than the R129's. For an even greater blend of open air and saloon-like comfort, the R230 would soon to be made available with a glass version of the Vario roof, which lent the interior a wonderfully light and open feel even while it protected you from the elements.

Regardless of whether the Vario roof was open or closed, the interior of the new SL was defended, like the old one, by an automatic roll-over bar that sprang upwards in less than

The SLK-like 'Vario' roof gave the SL the best possible blend of open roadster and snug coupé. The roof folded away in just sixteen seconds.

Like the old R129, the new SL had an automatic roll-bar that flipped up in an emergency. Unlike the old model, the new car was strictly a two-seater.

Like all Mercedes cars the SL was subjected to the 'roof drop test'. The windscreen pillars are severely tested – but the SL came through with flying colours.

0.3 seconds if its sensors detected that the car might roll. Alternatively the driver could opt to raise the roll bar hydraulically, the system stealing its power from the Vario roof's hydraulic pump.

Inside, buyers were given the choice of traditional wood-and-leather trim with a choice of three different wood finishes (chestnut, burr walnut and black ash), or a more contemporary matt-aluminium finish. Fewer people noticed the new polyurethane sheeting, which formed the surface of the dashboard panel and which was mostly applied and trimmed by hand. Ahead of the driver sat two heavily cowled main instruments, with 'retro' satin-chrome surrounds and chronograph-watch styling for their dials. Inset into the bottom of the dials were oval, digital displays providing

warning messages and information, which even included tyre pressure data relayed by radio from sensors at each wheel. Warning lights were arranged in arcs within the main gauge faces, while temperature and fuel contents were monitored via minor gauges flanking the main dials. It all added up to a clear and attractive method of providing plenty of data for the driver without overloading the dashboard with instruments.

As before, the seats carried the seat-belt mountings to ensure that the belts were presented in exactly the right positions for the occupants. The seats themselves had now been

The clear instrument-panel features styling inspired by chronograph watch design. Note the tyre pressure monitor in the lower part of the tachometer.

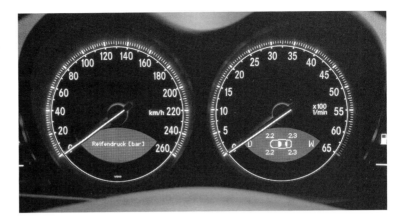

developed to provide extra comfort by incorporating 'active ventilation', a battery of tiny cooling fans that drew air through the seat – a feature first seen on the S-class saloon. As usual there were heating elements for colder weather and multi-way electrical adjustment. The most significant feature was that there were only two seats, the minimal rear seats of the R129 having been dispensed with, and instead the focus had been on providing more space for the front seats. For years ergonomics experts had known that the population was getting taller and Mercedes-Benz had designed the R230 for the average size of driver expected in 2005. Legroom, headroom and elbow-room were all more generous than before, as was in-cabin stowage space: there were two lockable storage boxes sitting behind the seats, neat door pockets and even a glove box that was bigger than before.

Occupant safety had also taken another step forward, with a new two-stage activation system for the driver and passenger air-bags, new 'head and thorax' air bags inside the doors and seat-belt force limiters to avoid injuries caused by the belts themselves. Mercedes-Benz also offered the optional Teleaid system, which would automatically alert emergency services if the car was involved in a crash and guide them to the scene using satellite navigation technology.

As before, the seat belts were mounted on the seats and there was now more room for the driver and passenger.

Fans buried inside the seats provided 'active' ventilation.

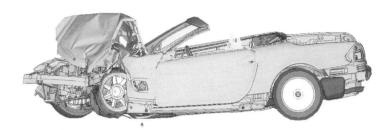

High-power computers now assist in many aspects of car design. Computer models helped analyse the crash performance of the SL bodyshell, long before the first prototypes had been built.

Braking by Wire

The R230 SL saw the series-production debut of an amazing new braking system, which had been revealed six months earlier and which Mercedes-Benz called Sensotronic Brake Control or SBC. Sensotronic controlled the brakes electronically, rather than mechanically as in a conventional brake system. Brake fluid was held in a high-pressure accumulator and supplied to the brake system at up to 160bar (over 2,000psi) under the control of a computer system that constantly calculated the optimum brake pressure required at each wheel. Under emergency braking the system could spot when the driver suddenly switched from accelerator pedal to brake pedal: it instantly raised the pressure in the brake system and moved the brake pads close to the discs so that full brake force could be applied the moment the driver applied the brakes.

Not that the benefits of the system ended there. In wet conditions Sensotronic applied the brakes gently at intervals to clear water from the discs, ensuring that efficient braking would be there the moment the driver needed it. Sensotronic could recognize when the SL was braking in a bend, increasing the braking force on the more heavily loaded outer wheels while reducing the amount of braking on the lightly loaded inner wheels – thus giving each tyre the level of braking it could deal with. A side-effect was to introduce some stabilizing understeer if the driver chose to brake in a bend. As on the previous SL and other Mercedes models, there was an Electronic Stabil-

Despite the use of computers, crash testing is still a vital tool and is essential for official approval of a car's safety features. The SL easily passed the required front- and side-impact tests.

ity Program (ESP) built into the braking system, which could brake one or more wheels independently to correct the car's attitude if it should slide in fast cornering, and an Acceleration Skid Control (known by its German abbreviation ASR), which cut power and applied the brakes if necessary to quell wheelspin during acceleration. At the other end of the speed scale, a 'soft stop' feature was incorporated that ensured that the SL would always come to a stop gently in city traffic, a 'start assist' function prevented the car from rolling back on hills and a 'tailback assist' feature could be selected to brake the car to a standstill every time the throttle was released. As on the R129, Brake Assist was incorporated to ensure that full brake pressure was used in an emergency stop and there was the now-ubiquitous anti-lock system. But now activation of the ABS no longer caused the brake pedal to vibrate under the driver's foot as a warning: tests at DaimlerChrysler's driving simulator in Berlin had shown that almost two thirds of drivers were startled by the vibration of the pedal as the ABS cut in and reacted by lifting off the pedal – thus extending their stopping distance in an emergency situation.

Citroën had used high-pressure hydraulics in their braking systems for models such as the DS and SM years before and their system had demonstrated one of the drawbacks: the Citroën brake 'pedal' was a push-button on the floor which required the driver's foot to apply pressure, but little movement. To many drivers this felt alien and it interfered with their smooth control of the brakes. To avoid the same problem with Sensotronic, Mercedes used a conventional brake pedal that was given artificial 'feel' using spring and hydraulic pressure. In the unlikely event that the car's electronic systems failed, the brake pedal auto-

Side airbags supplemented the usual front airbags, for maximum occupant protection in the event of a collision.

Drive-by-Wire

Mercedes-Benz calls it 'Mechatronics', the blending together of mechanical and electronic systems to provide better control and additional functions. You and I would call it drive-by-wire.

Modern aircraft already incorporate numerous 'fly-by-wire' systems that make the pilot's life easier. Think of the control surfaces on the wings or tail of an airliner or fighter plane: clearly at high speeds the loads on those control surfaces would be impossible for the pilot to handle, so the control surfaces have to be powered. The complex mechanical systems controlling the power assistance can now be replaced by electronic systems and all the pilot needs to do is send commands to the electronics, which decide the best way to carry out the pilot's wishes.

Drive-by-wire systems apply similar technology to cars. Instead of pulling open a throttle valve with a Bowden cable, a drive-by-wire throttle pedal sends a signal to the engine management system. The engine management computer establishes the throttle pedal position, and perhaps calculates the speed at which the position is changing, and controls the engine accordingly – not just opening the throttle, but perhaps also increasing turbocharger or supercharger boost pressure, altering ignition and fuelling settings and changing the valve timing.

Brake-by-wire was the most controversial use of these mechatronic systems because of the safety aspects, but that is now a reality with the SL's Sensotronic system. It's likely that more and more systems in future will be controlled by electronics rather than mechanical systems: steer-by-wire will be next.

matically connected to a manual hydraulic system giving braking on the front wheels, so the car could still be brought safely to a standstill.

As standard, the big ventilated discs sat inside 8.5 × 17in wheels, but buyers could also choose from two styles of five-spoke 18in wheel, 8.5in wide at the front and 9.5in wide at the back and fitted with 255/40 and 285/35 tyres respectively.

New suspension and new steering controlled the wheel movements. The recirculating ball steering that had been a Mercedes favourite for so many years had been replaced by a rack and pinion system, which was lighter and more precise in its feel, and speed-sensitive power assistance was provided to make parking easy but still retain some feedback on the open road. The strut-type layout used at the front of the R129 had gone, replaced by a sophisticated four-link system combining aluminium and steel suspension links. At the rear the R230 used a new version of the multi-link axle that Mercedes had now adopted for all its road cars, but with a new innovation: for the first time the entire assembly was made from aluminium alloy, reducing its weight by about a third, and it was also more compact than before.

But the suspension layout itself was not the most exciting part of the SL's running gear, because the car was fitted with the Active Body Control (ABC) system that had made its debut on the CL-class coupé in 1999. ABC

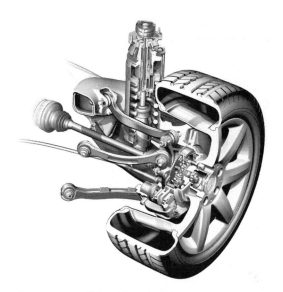

A more compact, lightweight multi-link suspension system was used at the rear.

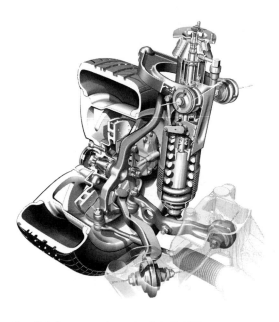

Four-link front suspension replaced the R129's strut-type layout.

supplemented the conventional springs and dampers with a fast-acting hydraulic cylinder at each wheel. Thirteen sensors placed around the car detected roll in cornering and pitch under braking, and the hydraulic rams could be activated to restore the body to a level position. Conventional anti-roll torsion bars connecting together the suspension arms on either side of the car were no longer necessary because the ABC system performed the same function, while the suspension dampers could be given much softer settings to improve the ride without affecting grip and handling. The practical result was that with ABC the SL's cornering was impressively flat and stable and, at the same time, there was a silky softness to the ride quality.

Engines and Ingenuity

After all the innovations of the R230's body, brakes and suspension, the two engine choices available at launch seemed a little ordinary. There were two models, an SL500 and an SL55

Mercedes racing driver Klaus Ludwig took part in final suspension tests on the SL.

Some of the suspension testing was carried out on the Hockenheim circuit. Here the still-secret SL wears camouflage over its headlights and badges.

AMG, both powered by V8 engines from the M113 family, which had already been seen in the R129 and in other Mercedes models. The SL500 had 306bhp from its 4,966cc V8, essentially the same engine that was fitted in the R129 SL500, but now with a smaller cooling-water volume for faster warm-up. The transmission was similar, with the same internal gear ratios, but the final drive was slightly shorter, to give fractionally better acceleration than the old SL500. Fuel economy was similar to the previous model.

The SL55 AMG, however, was a very different animal to the R129 that had borne that name. That had been powered by a long-stroke V8 with 354bhp, but the new one could make use of no less than 476bhp despite retaining the 5439cc capacity of the old car – making it (temporarily) the most powerful Mercedes-Benz series production car. The difference was due to the fitment of a screw-type supercharger between the cylinder banks, boosting at up to 0.8bar (about 9psi). The supercharger was made from two Teflon-coated cast-aluminium screws driven off the crankshaft by a poly-V belt at more than 23,000rpm when the

Hot weather testing proved the SL's engine and brake cooling, not to mention the air-conditioning system. Note how the shape of the rear lights has been disguised with tape.

157

V8 engines powered the first two models of the R230 line-up, but V6 and V12 engines would soon follow.

Boss of the Mercedes Car Group, Professor Jürgen Hubbert, at the launch of the SL55 AMG in 2001.

engine was at its peak, pushing up to 1,850kg of air per hour into the combustion chambers, but only when the engine management system deemed it necessary. The supercharger could be deactivated by an electromagnetic clutch, giving the SL55 AMG a part-time supercharging that recalled the driver-selectable supercharger of the SSK back in the thirties. Unlike the SSK, the SL55 AMG had an air-to-water charge air intercooler with its own 'low temperature' cooling-water circuit separate from that of the engine and the lower intake charge temperatures that resulted avoided any pre-

ignition problems, despite the V8 running a relatively high compression ratio of 9.0:1 (compared to 10.5:1 for the previous normally-aspirated engine).

Handling all the power was a five-speed automatic gearbox, which could be operated manually using Formula 1-style shift buttons on the steering wheel. The SL55 AMG also boasted uprated running gear to match its extra straight-line performance and more aggressive bodystyling so that everyone would know you had spent the extra 30,000 Euro (about £20,000) on the AMG version. Soon the supercharged V8 would find its way into the CL-class and S-class – and the SL would be given an even more powerful engine.

Sixes and Twelves

Mercedes expanded the SL range in 2002 with the announcement of new engine options at both ends of the range: at the bottom there was now a 3.7-litre V6-engined SL350, while the SL range was now crowned with a new king, a new V12-engined SL600 – and Mercedes-Benz took the opportunity to point out that it was the world's largest manufacturer of passenger-car V12s.

The new four-lamp face of the SL was more penetrating than before, while still being clearly a Mercedes shape.

The side-vents are a strong reminder of previous SLs.

Clever aerodynamics meant that, even with the top down, the R230's cabin remained calm at speed.

The R230's profile was much more interesting than the rather slab-sided R129.

Even though the SL350 still cost more than £57,000 in the UK, it was very much an entry-level model, lacking the expensive ABC suspension that gave the other SLs such an extraordinary blend of roll-free cornering and ripple-free ride. Instead it relied on a more conventional 'passive' suspension, with roll control provided by an anti-roll bar at each end. There was nothing intrinsically wrong with this conventional suspension system, but the SL350's road manners could not match those of its bigger-engined brethren with their computer-controlled responses.

Under the bonnet was a development of the three-valve V6 engine previously seen in the R129, having taken over from the old in-line six in the SL280 and SL. Now it was expanded in bore size until it had the same dimensions as the V8, with a 97mm bore and 84mm stroke,

The SL55AMG was adopted as the safety car for Formula 1 events, an important safety role requiring a high-performance vehicle.

Active Body Control suspension controlled roll in corners and gave the SL a remarkably refined ride.

In 2002 Mercedes added two new SL models – a V12 SL600 and this, the V6 SL350.

Production of all SL models continues at the Bremen plant.

but with only six cylinders it was smaller, at 3724cc – despite the '350' designation. With more torque and more power than the old SL320, it was significantly quicker and performed with the kind of refinement that buyers in this class had come to expect.

They could expect even more refinement from the V12 SL600 that now topped the range. It was a new engine, a little smaller than before (5513cc rather than 5987cc) and now utilizing the three-valve and dual alternating-current ignition technology that had helped the latest generation V6 and V8 engines to deliver such an impressive blend of power, economy and emissions performance. More important for the headline power figures was the addition of a pair of turbochargers, one for each cylinder bank, each with its own air/water intercooler, which could reduce intake charge temperatures by as much as 100°C. The long V12 was based around a diecast aluminium crankcase containing an immensely strong forged-steel crankshaft and steel conrods, which were forged in one piece and then fractured across the big end: when the two pieces were bolted together again the

complex mating surface of the fracture gave the component enormous strength. Hollow, induction-hardened steel camshafts and a diecast aluminium sump contributed to the engine's remarkably low weight of 578lb (263kg).

Apart from minor trim and specification differences, the SL600 was much the same as the other SLs in other respects, though the braking

As always the SL attracts the rich and famous – like German tennis star Boris Becker.

R230	
Chassis and body	Unitary steel body. Aluminium alloy bonnet, boot lid, doors and front wings
Engine	Front engine, longitudinal
Designation	SL350: M112 E35
	SL500: M113 E50
	SL55 AMG: M113 E55
	SL600: M275 E55
Block material	Aluminium alloy
Head material	Aluminium alloy
Cylinders	SL350: V6
	SL500/SL55 AMG: V8
	SL600: V12
Cooling	Water
Lubrication	Wet sump
Bore × stroke	SL350/SL500: 97.0 × 84.0mm
	SL55 AMG: 97.0 × 92.0mm
	SL600: 82.0 × 87.0mm
Capacity	SL350: 3724cc
	SL500: 4966cc
	SL55AMG: 5439cc
	SL600: 5513cc
Main bearings	SL350: 5
	SL500/SL55 AMG: 5
	SL600: 7
Valves/operation	Twin chain-driven overhead camshafts per cylinder bank
	SL350: 18 valves
	SL500: 24 valves
	600SL/SL600: 36 valves
Compression ratio	SL350/SL500: 10.0:1
	SL55 AMG/SL600: 9.0:1
Fuel system	Bosch fuel injection
Maximum power	SL350: 245bhp @ 5,700rpm
	SL500: 306bhp @ 5,600rpm
	SL55 AMG: 476bhp @ 6,100rpm
	SL600: 500bhp @ 5,000rpm
Maximum torque	SL350: 258lb ft @ 3,000–4,500rpm
	SL500: 339lb ft @ 2,700–4,250rpm
	SL55 AMG: 516lb ft @ 2,650–4,500rpm
	SL600: 590lb ft @ 1,800–3,600rpm
Transmission	Rear-wheel drive
	SL350: Six-speed 'Sequentronic' semi-auto standard, five-speed auto optional
	SL500/SL55 AMG/SL600: Five-speed automatic standard
Type	Five-speed automatic
Gear ratios (1-2-3-4-5-R)	3.59-2.19-1.41-1.00-0.83-3.16
Coupling	Torque converter
Final-drive ratio	SL500/SL55 AMG: 2.82:1
	SL600: 1.93:1
Type	Six-speed 'Sequentronic'
Final-drive ratio	3.27:1

R230 *continued*	
Suspension and steering	
Front	Four-link, coil springs
	SL350: Anti-roll bar
	SL500/SL55 AMG/SL600: ABC level control
Rear	Multi-link, coil springs, telescopic dampers
	SL350: Anti-roll bar
	SL500/SL55 AMG/SL600: ABC level control
Steering	Recirculating ball with power assistance
Wheels	8.5J × 17
Tyres	Radial, 255/45R17
Brakes	Disc brakes, ventilated and cross-drilled at front, with Sensotronic Brake Control system. Anti-lock and Brake Assist.
Dimensions	
Length	176in (4,470mm)
Width	71.3in (1,811mm)
Height	51.3in (1,303mm)
Track – front	60.4in (1,534mm)
Track – rear	60in (1,524mm)
Wheelbase	99.0in (2,515mm)
Unladen weight	SL350: 3,870lb (1,755kg)
	SL600: 4,300lb (1,950kg)
Fuel tank capacity	17.6gal (80ltr)
Performance	
Top speed	Electronically limited to 155mph (250km/h)
Acceleration	0–62mph (100km/h)
	SL350: 7.2sec
	SL500: 6.3sec
	SL55 AMG: 4.7sec
	SL600: 4.7sec

system did incorporate another feature that was at the forefront of new technology. The discs themselves were made from a carbon-fibre-reinforced ceramic material, which was said to combine instant response with the ability to resist temperatures of up to 1,000°C, minimizing brake fade. The carbon ceramic discs were also said to last longer – up to 185,000 miles (300,000km) – and weighed 60 per cent less than conventional grey cast-iron discs.

Latest Developments

Mercedes-Benz has now upgraded the transmissions of the SL500 (along with the E500, S430, S500 and CL500), installing the new 7G-TRONIC gearbox. 7G-TRONIC is the first seven-speed automatic gearbox to be offered for passenger cars by any manufacturer and Mercedes-Benz claim it offers performance and fuel economy benefits. Smoother gear shifting is said to be another plus point and the new transmission speeds downshifts by missing out gears rather than sequentially selecting every gear during deceleration or kickdown. Thanks to a lightweight magnesium-alloy casing, the new seven-speed gearbox is only fractionally heavier than the five-speeder automatic it supplants.

The new 3.5-litre, four-valve V6 engine

SLs of the Future

What lies ahead for R231, the replacement for the current SL, which should debut around 2008? Perhaps the best clue comes from Mercedes' F500 Mind research vehicle, which made its debut at the Tokyo show late in 2003. While the F500 is a four-seater saloon, much of the technology it embodies could find its way into future SL generations.

The F500 Mind was unveiled at the Tokyo show in 2003.

Innovations shown on Mercedes-Benz's F500 Mind concept car may be seen in future generations of the SL.

One such innovation concerns the pedals. F500 maximizes its interior space by using electronic accelerator and brake 'pedals', which are actually pressure-sensitive pads. Because the pedals do not move, less space is needed in the footwell, allowing greater legroom and more efficient packaging of the vehicle. The non-moving pedals will also reduce lower-limb injuries in accidents. The biggest challenge for the Mercedes-Benz engineers will be to 'tune' the pedal response so that drivers can accept and understand the system, unlike the Citroën brake 'button', with which many could not cope.

F500 also incorporates features to make driving easier and safer, including a long-range 'night vision' display using laser headlights and a 'multivision' display system, which delivers information to the driver in a flexible and fatigue-reducing way using a multi-functional, programmable instrument display. Both these features seem likely to appear on future SLs, as does F500's use of the steering wheel to house buttons and controls as on a modern racing car.

More controversial, perhaps, might be the appearance of an F500-style powertrain in the SL. F500 is powered by a diesel hybrid unit combining the 250bhp V8 diesel from the S-class with a 68bhp (50kW) electric motor that takes over in stop-start conditions. With diesel engines improving all the time in refinement, could the next generation SL have diesel or even electric power under its bonnet? Will hybrid powertrains become more widely accepted or perhaps even essential, as cities struggle to cope with emissions and natural resources dwindle still further? Perhaps, but what is certain is that the next SL will embody the very latest in automotive technology – and promises to be as exciting and innovative as every SL has been, right back to 1952.

that made its debut in the R171 SLK is likely to find its way into the SL at some point, replacing the less powerful 3.7-litre three-valve V6 currently fitted in the SL350. The new V6 develops its extra power thanks to variable valve-timing for the exhaust cams in addition to the intakes, a world first, and it is likely that the same technology will, at some point, be applied to the V8 engines in face-lifted SL500 and SL55 AMG models.

Before then, though, there will be a new 'ultimate' SL. AMG (which, remember, is

Next-Generation SLK

A new R171 SLK debuted during 2004, with styling which reflects that of the R230 SL and the F1-inspired SLR-McLaren. R171 will be the first SLK available with a V8 engine, the existing V6 SLK32 AMG being dropped in favour of an SLK55 AMG with 476bhp and fitted with the new 7G-TRONIC seven-speed automatic transmission.

The entry-level model is now the SLK200 Kom-

The new SLK, launched in 2004, features SLR-like styling.

pressor, with 163bhp from a 2.0-litre supercharged in-line four. Between this and the SLK55 AMG lies the SLK350, with a new V6 engine featuring variable intake and exhaust-valve timing and four valves per cylinder, giving it a punchy 272bhp. Both the SLK200 Kompressor and SLK350 are fitted with six-speed manual gearboxes as standard, with autos as options – five-speed on the four-cylinder model, seven-speed on the V6.

The new SLK boasts a wider track than before, with revised multi-link suspension at the rear and a new 'three-link' front suspension design. The result should be higher levels of grip and enthusiasts are hoping that the new SLK will also be a more sporting drive than the old car.

R171 boasts class-leading aerodynamic efficiency, improvements to performance and fuel economy, and a host of new or improved convenience features, such as the revised Vario roof that first saw service on the R230 SL. It has plenty to offer and should prove just as successful as the outgoing R170 SLK, which sold more than 300,000 units between 1996 and early 2004.

now a DaimlerChrysler subsidiary) has already released a 612bhp V12 engine in the big CL65 AMG coupé and S65 AMG saloon and that engine will also appear in the SL. Though the 'CL65' and 'S65' designations suggest that the engine is a 6.5-litre, in fact it displaces 'only' 5980cc, up from the 5513cc of the standard V12 thanks to a marginally wider bore and a stroke increased by 6mm to 93mm. Maximum boost pressure has been raised to 1.5bar (22psi) and to ensure the engine can reliably stand the extra boost there are forged pistons and revised bearings. The engine is capable of producing up to 885lb ft (1,200Nm) of torque, but is electronically limited to 738lb ft (1,000Nm), apparently to preserve the gearbox.

As ever, the top speed of the car will be limited to a 'responsible' 155mph (250km/h), while the benchmark 0–62mph (100km/h) sprint will probably take less than 4.5sec, making what will no doubt be called the SL65 AMG the quickest SL ever made by the factory, though if that still is not quick enough for you Brabus will happily supply a 6.3-litre 640bhp V12 with a top speed of 192mph (310km/h). Either way, the SL will be quicker and more exciting than ever, trading punches with the best that the Italian supercar manufacturers can offer. And that's just what the SL, in all its generations, has done for more than fifty years.

9   Owning an SL

From rare and ultra-valuable collectors' pieces, to affordable usable classics, to modern super-cars, the fifty years of SL-class Mercedes-Benz models offer a bewildering variety of sports cars and tourers. There are coupés and road-sters, snug hard-tops and versatile soft-tops, and accommodation for two, three or four. Engines range from 2.3-litre sixes to light-alloy V8s to turbocharged V12s, from 150bhp to more than 500bhp.

As if that wasn't enough there's also the 'junior series' to consider – the 1950s 190SL in roadster and hard-top form, and the more recent SLK-class with its clever folding roof. With so many different machines to choose from, how do you work out which is for you?

Classic or Modern?

Automotive technology has improved immea-surably in recent years, so even a car that was advanced for its time will be showing its age forty years later – in some areas, at least. Don't expect your 'Pagoda-roof' 230SL to offer the same kind of refinement or grip or perfor-mance as a modern Mercedes, and don't expect a 1960s car to cope with the minimal servicing a modern machine requires; some servicing may be needed as often as every 1,000 miles.

Parts can often be a headache for an old car, but classic SL owners are better-served than many classic car enthusiasts. Mercedes-Benz's policy of supplying parts for its older models makes keeping these cars on the road much easier than it is for some marques; that can mean that a classic Mercedes-Benz is a more practical proposition than an older model from some rival makers.

The relatively small numbers of parts pro-duced for the older cars inevitably means that they aren't cheap. As a result there are often replica or 'pattern' parts available, which are much cheaper to buy, but tend to compromise on materials or manufacture – and that can mean they work out no cheaper in the long run. Wear items like brake pads may not last as long, for example, so in the long term they require replacing more often – incurring additional labour charges. Pattern body-panels are often

Older SLs cannot match new cars for refinement or performance, but they have a charm and appeal all their own.

166

Though superseded, the R129 SL still offers technology way beyond most cars on the road.

Mercedes-Benz parts are still available for many classic models.

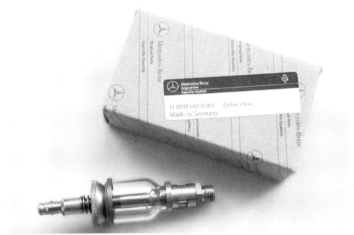

poorly shaped, needing time-consuming attention from an experienced panel beater before they will fit adequately. It can be cheaper simply to buy the higher-quality original equipment panel that fits much better to start with.

Another problem can be what fuel to run these earlier cars on. Engines built for leaded fuel are susceptible to valve-seat damage if driven hard on unleaded fuels, which are now almost universal as a result of concerns about the environmental impact of lead in the atmosphere. Fortunately, additives are available that perform the same function as the lead compounds in leaded fuel and engine modifi-

cations can be carried out as part of a normal top-end engine overhaul, which then allow the engine to run happily on an unleaded diet.

But the inevitable drawbacks of running a car that might have been built four or five decades ago are balanced by unique advantages. Classic cars are antiques of our time, but at the same time can still earn their keep. You're unlikely to use one of the race-bred 300SL Gullwing or Roadster models on a daily basis simply because of their value, but certainly the 'Pagoda-roof' models or the R107 from the 1970s and 1980s are well able to cope with daily use.

Drive a classic Mercedes and you will stand out from the crowd – most of the time.

Run one of these classic SLs every day and you will certainly stand out from the crowd, and for many people one of the main attractions of running a classic is their styling – here the SLs excel, all of them having stylish and confident shapes. You will also find other drivers often treat owners of classics with more respect and good humour than they do the drivers of modern sports cars.

What to Look For

SLs of all eras are sophisticated machines that need careful maintenance and, as we've already seen, this is particularly the case for the earlier machines, which need much more frequent servicing. Whatever the age of the SL you are looking at, it's essential that there is evidence of proper scheduled maintenance and swift attention to any necessary repairs.

For a recent machine the ideal is a fully-stamped service book showing work by a Mercedes-Benz main dealer, but classic SLs are less likely to still be maintained within the official dealer network. There are many independent Mercedes-Benz specialists, often employing factory-trained mechanics, and some of them specialize in the SL models – giving them a head start when it comes to diagnosing obscure problems with the older cars. Whether work has been done by a Mercedes dealer or an independent marque specialist, the important point is that servicing has been regular and thorough.

A reassuring wad of receipts and service records accompanying an older car should give you all the evidence you need that the car has been properly maintained. Check that the dates and mileages noted on the receipts progress in an orderly fashion and if there are long gaps where nothing seems to have been done try to find out why. Also look for the use of original equipment Mercedes-Benz parts rather than pattern parts, which shows, if nothing else, that little expense has been spared on maintenance.

It's also good to see a Mercedes-Benz Classic Certificate amongst the car's paperwork, for two reasons. First, the certificate is accompanied by a run-down of the car's specifications when it was built, which can show how original its current condition is. Second, the purchase of the certificate suggests that the owner was interested in his car and that tends to mean it will have been better cared for.

As far as the vehicle's condition goes, each model is different and we will take each one in turn. But there are some common areas that apply to most of the SLs. On roadsters the condition of the hood is vital, for instance. A leaky soft-top will allow water into the car, potentially ruining the interior trim (which is expensive to replace on all models) and also allowing moisture to attack the floor and sill panels. If these are weakened due to corrosion the whole structural integrity of the car is compromised.

Running gear and engines are generally strong and long-lasting and, in many cases, are shared with contemporary Mercedes-Benz saloons, so parts are relatively common.

Regular servicing is vital for all SLs. Examine the car's history file closely to ensure that routine maintenance has been carried out.

Buying a 190SL

Today the 190SL still fulfils the same function it did when it was new: it offers a taste of a 300SL at a much more affordable price, though the gap between their values has widened somewhat since the 1950s. Back then a 190SL was a little over half the price of a 300SL, while today a good example fetches up to £20,000, which is around a tenth the value of a 300SL.

Rust is the biggest enemy. Fortunately the alloy doors, boot lid and bonnet are not susceptible to corrosion, but the main steel-structure definitely is. The condition of the floor and sills is most important because they provide much of the car's structural strength. Repairs are possible, though Mercedes-Benz parts are expensive. Mechanically there is little to worry about, with strong engines and running gear.

Performance is leisurely by modern standards, thanks to a relatively low power-output and heavy body, but the 190SL is much more comfortable and convenient than many 1950s sports cars – and that makes it all the more appealing today.

The Spaceframe 300SLs

Prices have dropped since the mid-eighties, when speculators skewed the market to such an extent that only multi-millionaires and insurance companies owned the more desirable classic cars. But, even now, all the early spaceframe SLs are highly sought after and hugely valuable. At the time of writing a good Gullwing would fetch around £175,000, with exceptional cars and those with an interesting history (racing in the hands of a famous driver or ownership by a celebrity, for example) fetching even more. Roadsters are slightly less sought-after than the iconic Gullwings, with good cars around the £140,000 mark. Even cars requiring full restoration are likely to cost

The spaceframe 300SLs are expensive, but rewarding.

£50,000 or more and the restoration costs involved in returning them to their former glory will be astronomical.

Because of the sums involved in buying and restoring these early cars, it is vitally important to get them checked out by a specialist before purchase. The factory-owned Mercedes-Benz Classic Centre at Fellbach, for instance, will inspect a car for a prospective purchaser for a fee of around £1,500, which is a small price to pay given the likely investment in the car itself.

The Classic 113- and 107-Series SLs

The biggest threat to the W113 'Pagoda' cars is their propensity to rust. Extensive protection against the ingress of moisture and road salt into dark corners of the bodywork only became a priority for manufacturers in the 1970s and any car of Pagoda's era needs to be

carefully examined before purchase to ensure the bodywork is free from corrosion. The most important areas to check are the cross-members behind the engine, the chassis rails, door sills, floor and the base of the A-pillars. It's especially important that the floor and sills are in good condition, because the SL, like many open-top cars, derives much of its structural strength from them.

As with most Mercedes-Benz cars, the engines pose few problems as long as they are maintained in accordance with the schedule: similar engines in Mercedes saloons regularly rack up high mileages – up to 200,000 miles (125,000km) and beyond – proving that the units are capable enough. An SL with that high a mileage is quite rare, however, as many of them tend to be pampered second cars that are not called upon to cover vast distances.

Values for the 'Pagoda-roof' SL currently range from around £10,000 for cars needing a lot of work, up to £30,000 for mint examples.

The W113 and R107 SLs make attractive classics.

The softer but quicker 280SL tends to fetch the highest prices and, curiously, the rare 250SL tends to fetch less than the 230SL.

The famed solidity of the 107-series cars is reflected in the numbers that survive and they generally survive in good condition. By the 1970s, corrosion protection was a more advanced art and the third-generation SL benefited from better protection – so corrosion problems will usually be restricted to items like the fuel pump (exposed under the car). On the mechanical side the news is good, provided the cars are maintained as per the service schedule. If oil changes are missed the timing chain and tensioner suffer, eventually causing the chain to jump, with valve/piston contact as the result. A common fault is a smoky exhaust caused by worn valve-stem oil-seals, though these are easily replaceable using the correct tools.

Buying an SLK

Like other modern Mercedes-Benz cars, the SLK is a good bet provided it has been subject to regular maintenance. Take a look at the history file that should accompany the car,

looking for evidence of regular servicing at a Mercedes dealer or specialist.

The 230 Kompressor engine is the one most people will aim for, as it offers more performance than the 200K and almost as much as the 320 V6. For those who want smooth refined progress, the V6 offers the obvious alternative to the sometimes intrusive whine of the supercharger on the four-cylinder cars.

While it is not as special to drive as some rival sports cars, the SLK does offer a convenient, stylish package and the Vario roof means it is a better blend of open roadster and closed coupé than any other car on the road – except an R230 SL.

The Latest R129 and R230 SLs

These are nearly-new cars, of course, and given their mechanical and electrical complexity it is vital that maintenance has been carried out according to the Mercedes-Benz recommended schedule. If the service history is sketchy, the best bet is to get the car inspected by a Mercedes specialist – and ideally given a full service before sale. Failing that, the first job after purchase should be a thorough service.

Modern R129 and R230 SLs offer style and high performance.

The R129s are available with a wide variety of engines, all of them efficient and powerful, but each offering a different balance between power and fuel economy. The 300 is the oldest and cheapest of them, while the 300SL-24 offers greater performance with little fuel-consumption penalty (though it does have a reputation for eating head-gaskets). When the V6s arrived they offered similar performance to the outgoing straight sixes, but with better fuel consumption. At the top end, the 500 and 600 offer much the same performance: the difference is that the 500 uses less fuel and is cheaper to service, while the 600 is even more refined and effortless. Check specifications carefully when buying, because quite fundamental equipment – such as air conditioning – was optional on most models.

So far the R230s have a smaller range of engines – the 3.7-litre V6, 5.0-litre and 5.4-litre V8s, and the twin-turbo 5.5-litre V12. The AMG-prepared V8 is marginally the quickest of them, though as with the R129 the V12 engine appeals for its effortless performance and aristocratic soundtrack. But even the 'entry level' V6 is impressively flexible, quiet and quick.

Whichever SL you go for, you are buying into one of the most successful lines of sports cars ever created – a family that stretches back to the 1950s and which has its roots in motor sport. No matter which model of SL you drive, it represents a level of innovation, engineering excellence and glamorous good looks that other sports car manufacturers can only dream of.

Mercedes-Benz Clubs

The oldest Mercedes-Benz club of all is not in Germany, nor in America, but in Britain. The Mercedes-Benz Club Ltd was set up in 1952 and now boasts a membership of some 2,700, who own Mercedes vehicles from throughout the marque's history. Club members receive a monthly colour magazine, the *Gazette*, and a variety of benefits including parts discounts, events and technical advice.

The Mercedes-Benz Club of America started out as a branch of the British club and is now the largest Mercedes club in the world, with more than 26,000 members. Both are now recognized by the Mercedes-Benz Car Club International, the factory organization set up to look after Mercedes clubs around the world, which is affiliated to just one club in each country – except Germany, for historical reasons, and Australia where each of the six federal states has its own club.

In Britain there is a second major Mercedes organization, the Mercedes-Benz Owners' Association, which offers its own benefits and events and produces a monthly colour magazine called *Mercedes Owner*.

Mercedes-Benz Club

Vic Harris
18 Viga Road
Winchmore Hill
London N21 1HJ
Telephone 020 8482 4892
www.mercedes-benzownersclub.co.uk

Mercedes-Benz Owners' Association

Langton Road
Langton Green
Tunbridge Wells
Kent TN3 0EG
Telephone 01892 860925
www.mercedesclub.org.uk

Mercedes-Benz Club of America

1907 Lelaray Street
Colorado Springs
CO 80909-2872
Telephone (719) 633-6427 8am to 5pm Monday to Friday (MST)
www.mbca.org

The Mercedes-Benz Classic Centre in Fellbach houses workshops that can restore SLs and other classic Mercedes cars to as-new condition. The SSK on the wall has its exhaust pipes exiting from the 'wrong' side of the bonnet, but it's a long story....

Mercedes-Benz officially recognizes one club in each country and puts on its own events for classic Mercedes owners.

10 Back to the Future – the SLR-McLaren

Mercedes-Benz unveiled a dazzling new show car at the North American International Auto Show in Detroit in January 1999. Billed as 'Tomorrow's Silver Arrow', the Vision SLR was the first public appearance of a project that would spend a further four years in development and would combine the engineering strengths of DaimlerChrysler, AMG and Mercedes-Benz's Formula 1 partner McLaren. The result would be unveiled late in 2003 as the Mercedes-Benz SLR McLaren, a supercar of simply awesome specification.

For some people the name was enough to get the juices flowing. The previous Mercedes SLR had been an advanced racing sports car with a successful, but tragically short, career in the hands of such greats as Juan Manuel Fangio and Sir Stirling Moss. But the new SLR was more than just a styling study with a name that echoed past achievements and lines that recalled a famous old racing car. The Vision SLR was the start of a new production-car project that would marry road- and racing-car technology together like no car since the original 300SL of the 1950s.

In the summer of 1999, DaimlerChrysler and McLaren announced that they had reached an agreement to jointly design and develop an SLR road car from the Vision SLR concept. Also, uniquely for a Mercedes, the car would be built in England – at a new McLaren Technology Centre that was then under construction at Woking, in Surrey. A few months later, at the Frankfurt Motor Show in September, a second Vision SLR concept car was revealed to the public – this time a roadster with SLK-like twin roll-over bars behind the seats.

The Original SLR: 1954–55

After the retirement of the racing 300SL from competition at the end of 1952, the Mercedes-Benz racing team concentrated on building a new Grand Prix car, the W196. Using some of the lessons learned from the 300SL, the W196 was based around a tubular spaceframe chassis and was given an in-line engine mounted at an angle to keep the car's centre of gravity low. The engine carried a development of the direct fuel-injection system that had been planned for a later version of the SL. But there was far more to the engine – designated M196 – than simply a novel fuel system.

The engine was designed for the new Formula 1 rules, which dictated unsupercharged engines with capacities of less than 2.5 litres. In its construction M196 was a quite old-fashioned, with a light-alloy crankcase and forged-steel cylinders, with welded sheet-steel water jackets. The whole engine was split into two: the cylinders were in two pairs of four, with power taken from a central gear on the crankshaft, and the camshafts were driven from a central gear train, serving four valves on each side. In its layout it looked like one bank of the V16 BRM engine of 1951 and for the same reason: splitting the engine in two

The 300SLR racing car of the 1950s had a tragically short career.

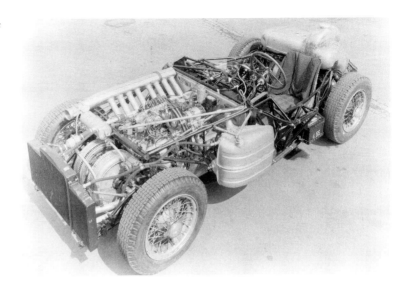

Original design drawings emphasize the styling relationship between the SLR and the 300SL.

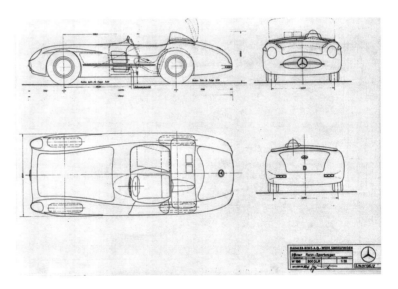

reduced the torsional vibrations to which the inevitably long crankshaft and camshafts would otherwise have been prone. The Hirth built-up crankshaft featured roller bearings both for the mains and big-ends.

At the top end there were two huge valves, but no valve springs. Conventional cams opening the valves were supplemented by a set of D-shaped cams which pulled the valves shut, this 'desmodromic' operation allowing the big, heavy valves to run at high lift and high speed without any danger of them colliding with the pistons due to valve bounce. Twin spark plugs, buried between the intake and exhaust ports, fired each cylinder.

At its debut in the French GP in July 1954, the W196 had 257bhp, enough to give Fangio pole position and the race win, with Kling second in another W196 and Hans Herrmann recording fastest lap in a third. Fangio went on to win the World Championship that year and again in 1955.

During 1954, a prototype sports car version of the W196 was developed and this W196S or 300SLR made its debut the following year (along with a gullwing version – *see* Chapter 3). To suit sports car racing regulations a 3.0-litre engine (M196/110) was built, this time using a cast cylinder-block, and the car revived another idea from the 300SL, the air brake – which meant it could compete with the disc-braked D-type Jaguars at Le Mans. Though the car proved fast, it was a season of mixed fortunes: Stirling Moss and Denis Jenkinson brilliantly won the Mille Miglia in a record time and Mike Hawthorn's Jaguar broke while chasing Fangio's SLR at the Tourist Trophy. After Pierre Levegh's solo performance at Le Mans a few years earlier, he was brought in to drive a 300SLR in the French classic. But early in the race Levegh's Mercedes tagged Lance Macklin's Austin-Healey, crashing into a 'safety' barrier, which launched the car into a packed grandstand. More than eighty spectators died, along with Levegh himself, in the most devastating accident motor racing has ever seen.

Much of the technology behind the 300SLR had been introduced on the earlier 300SL. The air-brake was particularly effective at high speeds, such as at Le Mans.

At the end of 1955 Mercedes-Benz withdrew from racing. We can only speculate on what the W196, in both its Formula 1 and sports car versions, might have achieved in the years that followed. Certainly the potential of the M196 engine was never remotely exploited, its famed docility and tractability being in part due to (typically Mercedes) conservative valve-timing, and further development was expected to push the power output of the Grand Prix engine beyond 400bhp. If the W196 had remained in competition, Ferrari's record in Formula 1, and Jaguar's at Le Mans, might have looked a lot different.

Moss and Jenkinson raced to a famous win in the Mille Miglia in 1955.

Original SLR

Chassis and body	Tubular steel spaceframe chassis with aluminium alloy body panels
Engine	Front engine, longitudinal, tilted right at 53 degrees to vertical
Designation	M196S
Block material	Silumin (in two blocks of four cylinders)
Head material	Silumin (cast en bloc with cylinders)
Cylinders	8 in-line
Cooling	Water
Lubrication	Dry sump
Bore × stroke	78 × 78mm
Capacity	2982cc
Main bearings	9
Valves/operation	Four chain-driven overhead camshafts, 16 valves, desmodromic operation
Compression ratio	9:1
Fuel system	Direct fuel injection, Bosch eight-plunger pump
Maximum power	310bhp @ 7,400rpm
Maximum torque	230lb ft @ 5,950rpm
Transmission	Five-speed manual gearbox with synchromesh on all forward ratios, mounted in unit with differential. Rear-wheel drive.
Gear ratios (1-2-3-4-5)	2.67-1.75-1.43-1.07-0.83
Clutch	Dry single-plate
Final-drive ratio	2.22:1 (others available from 3.15:1 to 2.17:1)
Suspension and steering	
Front	Double wishbones, torsion bars, telescopic dampers
Rear	Single-pivot swing axle, torsion bars, telescopic dampers
Steering	Worm-and-sector
Wheels	Centre-lock wire-spoke wheels, 6.00 × 16 front, 7.00 × 16 rear
Brakes	Hydraulically operated drum brakes all round, with finned light-alloy drums. Air-brake used at some races
Dimensions	
Length	169in (4,300mm)
Width	68.5in (1,740mm)
Height	43.3in (1,100mm)
Track – front	52.4in (1,331mm)
Track – rear	54.3in (1,379mm)
Wheelbase	93.3in (2,370mm)
Unladen weight	1,982lb (901kg)
Fuel tank capacity	58.3gal (265ltr)
Performance	
Top speed	Over 186mph (300km/h)
Acceleration	0–62mph (100km/h) approximately 7sec

Visionary View

The styling of the Vision SLR concept cars was intended to bring together a number of different influences. The headlight treatment and the Mercedes star were reminiscent of other Mercedes road cars – and in particular it gave a strong hint to the styling of the R230 SL, which was to be revealed a couple of years later, in 2001. The unconventional, upwards-opening doors were an echo of the 300SL

177

The Vision SLR show car of 1999 seen here was developed into the SLR-McLaren production car of 2003.

Gullwing, of course, though they operated on a different principle. The Vision SLR's frameless doors swung forwards at 75 degrees from a hinge on the A-pillar, much like the 'butterfly wing' doors of the Lamborghini Countach and Diablo – except that, in this case, the doors were electrically operated. Though undoubtedly an eye-catching feature, there was also a practical reason behind the choice: large conventional doors cannot be opened wide when the car is parked in a confined area.

Other influences to the styling came from Mercedes-Benz's motor sport involvement. The strong central rib to the bonnet and the low front-spoiler with its distinctive curved struts was designed to echo the appearance of the McLaren-Mercedes Grand Prix cars that had given Mika Häkkinen two world championships. But an influence from a long-departed era also revealed itself: the divided

side-vents and curved rear-end were strongly reminiscent of the 1950s SLR racing car.

The Vision SLR show-car's interior was dominated by a wide centre console that continued the lines of that prominent bonnet bulge into the interior. Either side of it were seats with carbon-fibre shells, the rest of the interior being kept simple with a classic twin-instrument facia, the dials themselves reminiscent of chronograph watch faces. Alcantara cloth dominated the cabin.

Based on an aluminium and carbon-fibre chassis, the Vision SLR was powered by a 557bhp V8 engine, a supercharged and intercooled version of the SL500 unit with the screw-type compressor and water-cooled intercooler fitted between the cylinder banks in the 'V' of the engine. DaimlerChrysler talked of a top speed around 198mph (320km/h) with a 0–62mph (100km/h) sprint time of 4.2sec.

The Vision SLR marked a return to the idea of 'gullwing' doors.

Front-end styling of the SLR was intended to mirror that of the successful McLaren-Mercedes F1 cars.

The low, sleek SLR-McLaren is capable of well over 200mph.

SLR Restyled

Early in 2000, a year after the Vision SLR study had first appeared, DaimlerChrysler announced that the production SLR was going to look a little different. Behind the scenes, conflicting concerns about crash performance, weight distribution and luggage space had prompted a revised layout, with the engine moved backwards in the chassis, giving the SLR surprisingly old-fashioned proportions with a rear-set cabin and a long bonnet.

But when the production-ready SLR was unveiled in 2003, it was clear that the basic ideas behind the styling of the original Vision SLR concept car had been retained and even,

in some cases, enhanced. The 'butterfly wing' doors with frameless windows had been replaced by doors that pivoted around the windscreen pillars, so that they opened upwards and outwards. The prominent bonnet bulge of the show car had been retained, while the 'Formula 1' front end had been revised to give the SLR a more penetrating appearance. The side vents had now been given additional vertical vanes, which made them resemble those of the 1950s SLR even more strongly. But the rear of the car was now less like its forebear: the downward-sloping bootlid of the show car had been replaced by a higher, more horizontal panel to reduce rear-end lift (as a side-effect giving the SLR a very spacious

The front end looks aggressive, even in this unusual dark colour. Most SLRs will probably be silver.

boot). Further aerodynamic subtleties, developed first on a scale model in the McLaren wind tunnel and later in a moving-floor tunnel in Stuttgart, were hidden underneath the car. The virtually smooth underbody reduced drag and race-car style diffusors at the front and rear axles managed the airflow to improve downforce at high speed.

Not that the connections with the old SLR had become any weaker, because, along the way, the new model had gained an air brake, something that had been a characteristic feature of the SLRs raced at Le Mans in 1955 (and was originally tried on the 300SL in 1952). 'Active' aerodynamics had always been a pet technology of McLaren designer Gordon Murray, too. In the 1970s, Murray devised the Brabham 'fan car', a Formula 1 machine that derived phenomenal grip and security in

corners from a huge fan at the back, which literally sucked the car down onto the road by creating a vacuum underneath. Murray's McLaren F1 road car of 1994 employed similar ideas to promote downforce. Now the Mercedes SLR was using active aerodynamics to help braking and stability at high speeds. Under control of a computer, a flap at the back of the car would rise to an angle of 10 degrees if the SLR was driven faster than 59mph (95km/h) and could be raised to an angle of 65 degrees when the driver braked heavily, to increase drag and aid stopping-power. A manual control was also provided to allow the driver to over-ride the computer's settings.

Under the skin, the SLR's construction was equally unconventional, with extensive use of Formula 1-style carbon-fibre structures. Two carbon-fibre composite cones, each about

Active aerodynamics help keep the SLR stable at high speed. F1-style diffusers under the back of the car generate downforce.

The SLR's rear spoiler raises automatically at speed and acts as an air brake when braking from high speed.

2ft (610mm) long and weighing 7.5lb (3.5kg), were bolted to the aluminium engine-mounts to control deformation of the front end of the car in a collision, the SLR being the first series production car with a carbon-fibre crumple zone. A carbon composite cell at the centre protected the occupants, while a further carbon crash structure protected the car from the rear. Side impacts were dealt with by carbon composite and aluminium structures in the doors, and by the high-strength carbon shells of the seats.

In racing car production, carbon composite structures such as these are made by hand, but the relatively high production volume of the SLR dictated a more mechanized approach. As a result, production systems were designed using such well-established textile techniques as knitting, sewing, weaving and braiding in a new context. The SLR's longitudinal members, for instance, were formed by making a web from several layers of carbon-fibre cloth, which were sewed together by machine, and then inserting this web into a machine that braided together 25,000 fine carbon-filaments to produce the required outer contour.

The SLR was equipped with the same sort of carbon-ceramic brake discs seen on the R230 SL and also incorporated the Senso-tronic 'brake by wire' system used on the SL and other high-end Mercedes cars. Enormous stopping power was generated by the eight-piston front calipers (acting on ventilated

The SLR is crammed with modern technology and achieves remarkable performance.

Instruments have 'McLaren' graphics, but will look familiar to R230 SL drivers.

The SLR cabin is trimmed in high-quality leather. The seat frames, like so much of the rest of the car, are carbon fibre.

370mm discs) and four-piston rears (acting on 360mm solid discs). Even the big brake lights were unconventional, using fifty-one LEDs each side instead of a conventional lamp, similar to the system used on the SL. The LEDs were said to have a longer service life than normal bulbs, and also reacted 150 milliseconds quicker.

More conventional was the SLR's suspension, using double wishbones, coil springs and telescopic dampers at both ends – though the anti-roll bar (at the front only) was operated by an F1-style pushrod system to keep the bar itself out of the way. Customers could choose from two designs of 18in wheels, a ten-spoke and a five-spoke, and 19in wheels were a further option.

Higher Power

Mercedes-Benz was a little coy about admitting it, but the SLR's motive power came from a development of the supercharged V8 engine from the SL55 AMG. The capacity was unchanged at 5439cc, but a higher compression ratio helped the power output rise from 476bhp to a colossal 626bhp (which was almost a coincidence, as the previous McLaren road car had 627bhp). Not only did the SLR match the performance predictions made for the Vision SLR show-car, it exceeded them by quite a margin, with a top speed well over 200mph (320km/h) and a 0–62mph (100km/h) acceleration time under four seconds.

Feeding the power to the rear wheels was

V8 engine develops 626bhp, just 1bhp less than the first McLaren road car – the F1 supercar of 1994.

the five-speed automatic gearbox familiar from other Mercedes models, but now with the option of selectable gearshift speed. The driver could select from 'Sport', 'SuperSport' or 'Race' settings, with progressively quicker but less well-cushioned changes. The gearbox could be left to change itself, or the driver could manually select gears using the selector lever or 'Touchshift' buttons on the steering wheel – just like a Formula 1 car.

The new SLR takes the carbon-composite structures, sophisticated aerodynamics and computer control of racing cars and applies it undiluted to the road. While the SL has developed into a sporting tourer rather than the true sports car it once was, with SLR Mercedes-Benz once again builds road cars with true racing technology – just like the 300SL of fifty years ago.

SLR-McLaren

Chassis and body	Carbon-fibre composite monocoque with carbon composite crash structures and aluminium subframes. Two upwards-opening doors hinged on the windscreen pillars
Engine	Front engine, longitudinal
Block material	Aluminium alloy
Head material	Aluminium alloy
Cylinders	V8
Cooling	Water
Lubrication	Dry sump
Bore × stroke	97 × 92mm
Capacity	5439cc
Main bearings	5
Valves/operation	Single overhead cam per bank, three valves per cylinder
Compression ratio	8.8:1
Fuel system	Computer-controlled fuel injection, screw-type supercharger and air/water intercooler
Maximum power	626bhp at 6,500rpm
Maximum torque	575lb ft at 3,250–5,000rpm
Transmission	Five-speed automatic gearbox. Rear-wheel drive.
Gear ratios (1-2-3-4-5-R)	3.56-2.19-1.41-1.00-0.83-3.56
Coupling	Torque converter
Final drive ratio	3.06:1
Suspension and steering	
Front	Double wishbones, coil springs, telescopic dampers, anti-roll bar
Rear	Twin-pivot swing axle, coil springs, telescopic dampers
Steering	Rack and pinion, power assisted
Wheels	9J × 18 front, 11.5J × 18 rear (9J × 19 front, 11.5J × 19 rear optional)
Tyres	245/40ZR18 front, 295 × 35ZR18 rear
Brakes	Electrohydraulic braking system with fail-safe hydraulic back-up system. Carbon-fibre-reinforced ceramic brake discs. Drum parking brake at rear. Anti-lock and brake assist systems. Computer-controlled air brake flap at rear with manual over-ride
Dimensions	
Length	183.3in (4,656mm)
Width	75.0in (1,905mm)
Height	49.7in (1,261mm)
Track – front	64.5in (1,638mm)
Track – rear	61.8in (1,569mm)
Wheelbase	106.3in (2,700mm)
Unladen weight	3,890lb (1,768kg)
Fuel tank capacity	21.5gal (97.6ltr)
Performance	
Top speed	207mph (334km/h)
Acceleration	0–62mph (100km/h) 3.8sec

SLR-McLaren Rivals

The SLR's performance puts it into a class where competition is relatively rare, and its combination of pace and practicality are hard to match. Porsche's mid-engined Carrera GT is a road-going version of a stillborn Le Mans racer that, like the SLR, is constructed entirely from carbon-fibre composite materials. Power comes from an all-alloy 68-degree V10 engine that develops 612bhp at 8,000rpm. Porsche claims a maximum speed of 205mph (330km/h) and a 0–62mph (100km/h) time of 3.9 seconds. It has the performance, then, to match the SLR – but the Carrera GT is very much a sports car rather than a GT and will appeal to a different set of customers.

Ferrari's new 612 Scaglietti is simply not as quick as the SLR, though it can offer an extra pair of seats as a compensation. Ferrari's fastest front-engined car, the 575M, still isn't quick enough – though the rare special edition Enzo could certainly show the SLR a clean pair of heels. But the short Enzo production run is sold out.

Ferrari's Italian rival Lamborghini produces cars that an SLR owner would not consider practical enough, but the mid-engined Murcièlago certainly rivals the SLR for pace. In Britain, Aston Martin produces true GT cars but, until a higher-performance version of the V12 Vanquish comes along, Newport Pagnell will have nothing that can catch the SLR.

Appendix – Cracking the Codes

Mercedes-Benz cars aren't always the easiest to correctly identify, because one model tends to share a lot of styling cues with the one before and the one after, and model designations tend to be recycled from one generation of cars to another. Often those designations are in themselves confusing, too, so pinpointing exactly which car it is you are dealing with can sometimes be tricky.

The basic system is logical enough, as you might expect from a German company with a reputation for sound engineering – but there are some curious exceptions to the rules. The number in the model designation – 230, 280, 350 and so on – denotes the car's engine size (2.3 litres, 2.8 litres or 3.5 litres respectively), though sometimes a larger engine was denoted with a capacity suffix rather than a change of code: the 450SL 5.0 is an example.

Originally Mercedes used letter codes to denote different models – SE, SL, SEL and so on. The S denoted sport or super, originally indicating a performance model. So, in the 1950s, a 300S was quicker than a plain 300. E stood for *Einspritzung* (German for injection), so a 1970s 230 is carburettored but a 230E is fuel-injected. C, as in SLC, means coupé. L can mean either *lang* (long, meaning long-wheelbase) or *leicht* (light), so a 450SEL is longer than a 450SE and a 300SL is lighter than a 300S.

But there the logic goes awry. SLs haven't really deserved the *leicht* tag for years and even though all but the 190SL and the earliest racing SLs have been fuel-injected they lack the *Einspritzung* 'E'. Strictly speaking the SLC is not a coupé because 'coupé' means cut short, and an SLC is longer than an SL.

Daimler-Benz Design Codes

The factory's own internal design numbers are some help in referring precisely to different models, though even here things are not as logical as it would appear: the numbers are not a simple chronological sequence.

Each one is prefixed with W for *Wagen* (car), R for roadster, C for coupé or S for station wagon. Occasionally P for prototype was also used, particularly on some of the pre-war race cars. Where there is more than one prefix for a number, it indicates there was more than one body style for the same basic vehicle – for instance, the R107 SL and closely-related C107 SLC. Engines have their own set of numbers prefixed with M for motor (*see* below). The codes are listed in chronological order.

M Codes: Engines

Until the 1960s a car and its engine were often given 'W' and 'M' codes with the same number – W196 is powered by M196, and so on. After that it became common for one class of car to be available with a variety of engines. For instance, the original 300SL was only available with one engine type and although

M159	2.6-litre in-line six, approximately 70bhp. Designed in 1930s but production prevented by the outbreak of war
M186	3.0-litre in-line six, 115bhp. Developed from M159 and used in 300 saloon from 1951
M188	3.0-litre in-line six. High-performance version of M186, used in range-topping 300Sm two-seater introduced in late 1951
M194	3.0-litre in-line six, approximately 170bhp. Much-developed racing version of M188 for use in W194 racing SL
M196	2.5-litre straight-eight engine for W196 Formula 1 car
M196/110	3.0-litre straight-eight. Also known as M196S. Sports car version of M196, used in 300SLR and Rudolf Uhlenhaut's 'Competition Coupé'
M197	3.0-litre straight-six. Supercharged version of M194, used in practice in the 300SL at the Nürburgring in 1952
M121	1.9-litre in-line four, three bearings, single OHC. 190SL engine, which also went into the *Ponton* saloon
M127	2.2-litre in-line six. SOHC. Used in 220SE, then enlarged for use in 230SL
M100	6.3-litre V8. Designed for the Mercedes 600 limousine, then used in the 300SEL 6.3 and a one-off experimental SL
M110	2.8-litre in-line six. Seven-bearings and twin OHC, used throughout the 1970s in many Mercedes models, including the R107 280SL
M116	3.5-litre V8. 'Short stroke' V8 first seen in 280SE 3.5, then used in R/C107 350SL/SLC (and the contemporary S-class saloon). Originally iron-block, but light-alloy block from 1985
M117	4.5-litre, 5.0-litre or 5.6-litre V8. Originally iron-block, but light-alloy block from 1985. Development of M116 allowing longer stroke for bigger capacity: the V8 used in R/C107 450SL and 560SL and then the R129 SL500 until 1998
M103	3.0-litre in-line six. Seven bearings, single OHC, used in R107 and R129 300SL models from 1985–93
M104	3.0-litre in-line six. Seven bearings, twin OHC, four valves per cylinder and variable intake-valve timing. Twenty per cent more power than the two-valve M103. Used in R129 300SL-24. Smaller bore and stroke created E28 version for SL280
M119	5.0-litre V8. Four valves per cylinder and variable intake valve timing. Developed from M117, introduced into SL500 in 1998
M120	6.0-litre V12 used in 600SL/SL600 R129
M111	2.0-litre in-line four. Five bearings, twin OHC, four valves per cylinder. The entry-level SLK engine
M112	2.8-litre and 3.2-litre V6s, replaced in-line M104 in the R129-series SL in 1998
M113	5.0-litre V8 introduced in R129 SL500 in 1998, and then carried over to R230 SL500
M275	Twin-turbo V12 in R230 SL600

W186	300 saloon, which formed the basis for the racing SL
W194	SL racing car 1952
W196	1954 Formula 1 car and the closely-related 300SLR racing car (W196S)
W198	300SL road car 1954–63. W198 I is the Gullwing, W198 II the Roadster
W120, W121	Family of cars including the *Ponton* saloon 1953–63. The 190SL roadster 1955–63, developed from *Ponton* saloon, is W121 B II.
W110, W111	'Fintail' saloon 1961–71.
W113	'Pagoda roof' SL 1963–70: 230SL, 250SL, 280SL. Developed from W110.
C107	SLC 1971–81: 280SLC, 350SLC, 380SLC, 450SLC, 450SLC 5.0, 500SLC
R107	*Panzerwagen* SL 1971–89: 250SL, 280SL, 450SL, 500SL, 380SL, 560SL
C126	SEC coupé 1981–91: 380SEC, 560SEC. Replaced the SLC class in 1981
R129	SL 1990–2002: SL280, SL300, SL320, SL500, SL600, SL60 AMG
R170	SLK 1998–2003: SLK200, SLK230K, SLK320, SLK32 AMG
R230	SL Class 2003 on: SL320, SL430, SL500, SL580, SL55 AMG
R171	SLK Class 2004 on: SLK180 KPI, SLK200 KPI, SLK220 KPI, SLK270 KPI, SLK30 AMG

there were three 'Pagoda-roof' SLs they ran consecutively – while subsequent SLs have been available with a range of engines. Also, engines began to be shared between the different Mercedes models – so in the 1970s the M110 2.8-litre engine not only powered the R/C107 280SL/SLC, but also the 280E saloon, 280CE coupé and 280TE estate (all from the W123 'mid-size' series), and the 280S/SE/SEL (all versions of the W116 'S-class' saloon) that were available at the same time.

189

Index